DEATH
The Final
Frontier

DALE V. HARDT, PH.D.

University of Wisconsin

DEATH
The Final
Frontier

PRENTICE-HALL, INC., ENGLEWOOD CLIFFS, NEW JERSEY 07632

Library of Congress Cataloging in Publication Data

Hardt, Dale V. 1946–
   Death, the final frontier.

   Includes bibliographies and index.
   1. Death—Psychological aspects. I. Title.
[DNLM: 1. Attitude to death. 2. Death. BF789.D4
H266d]
BF789.D4H37   301.42'86   78–6071
ISBN 0-13-197772-5 (c)
ISBN 0-13-197780-6 (p)

© 1979 by Prentice-Hall, Inc., Englewood Cliffs, N.J. 07632

Printed in the United States of America

10 9 8 7 6 5 4 3 2 1

Prentice-Hall International, Inc., *London*
Prentice-Hall of Australia Pty. Limited, *Sydney*
Prentice-Hall of Canada, Ltd., *Toronto*
Prentice-Hall of India Private Limited, *New Delhi*
Prentice-Hall of Japan, Inc., *Tokyo*
Prentice-Hall of Southeast Asia Pte. Ltd., *Singapore*
Whitehall Books Limited, *Wellington, New Zealand*

To my parents for their support, my wife for her support and help, and my son for his being.

To the students in my first death and dying classes at East Stroudsburg State College whose individualized efforts left me with a valuable bibliography.

Finally, to all those people who have touched my life and in doing so have given me a fuller existence. After all, it is only through life's experiences that we find the courage to face the inevitability of death.

Contents

Preface

Death may be described as "the new area of human concern," "the subject replacing sex in importance," even "the new obscenity." It is through our understanding of death and the death taboo that we can begin to appreciate the very life that is ours. Perhaps Dag Hammarskjold summed it up best when he said, "In the last analysis, it is our conception of death which decides our answers to all the questions that life puts to us." If we accept his premise, then death attitudes and their subsequent study are even more important than most writers suggest. Understanding our own attitudes regarding such matters as death and suicide is surely related to our ability to live a worthwhile and happy life.

Philosophers, theologians, and various groups of scientists have sporadically attempted to answer questions concerning death. It is often surprising how limited the literature is . . . until recently. In fact, from 1897 to 1970 only seventeen significant studies related to death attitudes were undertaken. Even fewer numbers of books were written on the subject apart from philosophical or theological theories. However, within the last five years much has been written because of increasing concern with the subject. It, too, is sporadic. And, unfortunately, most recent texts written in good, solid textbook form are for professionals or semi-professionals who deal with thanatological concerns. Admittedly, interest is there. There is, however, interest among high school and college-age individuals. Interest in the area can be identified by the rapid increase in death and dying courses in this country. Where do schools stand with respect to death education? In the past five years, education for death has been suggested by many authorities as a function of the schools. In other words, helping students come to terms with their fears and anxieties concerning death has become a concern of school systems.

If educators are to be concerned with education about death, they must also be aware of attitudes toward death. Education that concerns itself with student attitudes is more likely to fulfill students needs and interests. We are well aware that the attitudes an individual holds will influence the facts he is willing to accept. Thus, while attitudes alone may not determine how we react, they do play an influential part in this process.

Attitudes toward death comprise a complex area of concern with individual, subcultural, and cultural ramifications. Young children may experience the death of animals or pets and from this develop certain attitudes. However, it is questionable as to whether attitudes formed by experiences involving the death of animals and those involving the death of people are similar.

Because Americans try to prolong life at almost any cost, it can be deduced that most Americans fear death. Hence, among other coping mechanisms, repression of death thoughts is apparent. If we accept the premise that emotional health is partially dependent upon conscious awareness of our attitude toward death (and subsequent acceptance of death as a natural phenomena), then it follows that our attitude toward death constitutes an important part of the emotional foundations of our health.

It is hoped that this text will serve as a basis for reflection on information and issues, and that it will stimulate you to question your attitudes, beliefs, and practices toward death. The following list of questions is only a few of the many that you will hopefully contemplate as you make your way through the pages of this text.

How did our overall cultural perspective of death develop?

How much of a role did religion play and how much of a role does it continue to play in creating attitudes toward death?

How do our attitudes toward death and dying-related subjects compare with those found in research?

At what age did we first understand death as final and irreversible?

What is death?

How has it been defined?

Why do we define it as we do today?

How successful are various transplants?

Would I want a transplant if one were available?

Would I donate my body, or part of it, so another might live?

How does it feel to get old?

How do we treat our elderly?

Do I believe in euthanasia or mercy killing?

Have I ever considered suicide? (Does this make me different?)

How do other cultures, compared with ours, treat their dead?

Would I want to be buried, cremated, or be disposed of in other ways?

What do various religions, as well as my own, say about cremation, transplantation, and euthanasia?

How will I handle the death of my mother, father, or someone I love?

It is hoped that this text will help answer these and other questions and issues. The resolution of such questions and issues is dependent upon your involvement because this book does not attempt to provide *all* the answers. It may only suggest answers or alternatives, the final decision is yours.

Before beginning our discussion of attitudes toward death, measure yours. Following true experimental design, attempt to pre and post test your attitude toward death. I will not explain how to score the scale or what that score means now. Take the following test now. Then read this book and go through various classroom exercises. One to two weeks after you finish your class or this book, you should take the death attitude test again as it appears in Appendix B. Then you will learn how to score the death attitude scale and what your score means.

Death Attitude Scale: Pre-Test

The following items are not intended to test your knowledge. There are no right or wrong answers. Your responses are anonymous. *Directions:* Read each item carefully. Place a check mark next to each item with which you *Agree*. Make *No Marks* next to items with which you disagree.

249_____The thought of death is a glorious thought.

247_____When I think of death I am most satisfied.

245_____Thoughts of death are wonderful thoughts.

243_____The thought of death is very pleasant.

241_____The thought of death is comforting.

239_____I find it fairly easy to think of death.

237_____The thought of death isn't so bad.

235_____I do not mind thinking of death.

233_____I can accept the thought of death.

231_____To think of death is common.

229____I don't fear thoughts of death, but I don't like them either.

227____Thinking about death is over-valued by many.

225____Thinking of death is not fundamental to me.

223____I find it difficult to think of death.

221____I regret the thought of death.

219____The thought of death is an awful thought.

217____The thought of death is dreadful.

215____The thought of death is traumatic.

213____I hate the sound of the word death.

211____The thought of death is outrageous.

We are indebted to the following people for permission to reprint their material in this book:

ACS/NIH Organ Transplant Registry: Tables 1, 2, and 3; Allen, Robert A. and Richard Klofach: "Interview With a Funeral Director;" American Book (Van Nostrand Reinhold Co.): from "Mid-Winter Waking" by Robert Graves; American Medical Association: pp. 135-36, *Proceedings AMA House of Delegates*, Dec. 2-5, 1973; Reaffirmed p. 345, *Proceedings AMA House of Delegates*, June 23-27, 1974 and p. 303, Dec. 1-4, 1974. Reprinted by permission; Dodd, Mead & Company: from "The Cremation of Sam McGee" in *The Complete Poems of Robert Service* by Robert Service; Doubleday & Company, Inc.: "Grief" by Elizabeth Barrett Browning, "Prospice" by Robert Browning and "How Old Are You" by H. S. Fritsch from *Poems That Live Forever*; Euthanasia Educational Council, 250 West 57th Street, New York, New York, 10019: The Living Will. Reprinted with permission; Victor Gollancz Ltd.: quotation from *The Mighty and Their Fall* by Ivy Compton-Burnett; Hawthorn Books, Inc.: "St. Swithin" in *Harp in the Winds* by Daniel Henderson. Reprinted by permission; Houghton Mifflin Company: "The Law of Death" by John Hay from *Coloured Stars* by E. Powys Mathers; Kleintrup, Helen and the Eye Bank for Sight Restoration: Eye Donor Card; Alfred A. Knopf, Inc.: quotation from *Markings* by Dag Hammarskjold, translated by Leif Sjoberg and W. H. Auden; Lawrence, A. W.: quotation from *The Mint* by T. E. Lawrence. Reprinted by permission; Little, Brown and Company: quotation from *Comfort Me With Apples* by Peter DeVries, and "Time and Eternity" in *Poems* by Emily Dickinson, edited by Martha Dickinson Bianchi and Alfred Leete Hampson; MacMillan Publishing Co., Inc.: quotations from *On Death and Dying* by Elisabeth Kubler-Ross; *Oshkosh Daily Northwestern:* article dated December 10, 1975; The Owen Estate and Chatto & Windus: from "The Show" in *The Collected Poems of Wilfred Owen* by Wilfred Owen; G. P. Putnam's Sons: quotation from *Tell*

Dublin I Miss Her by Dominic Behan; Charles Scribner's Sons: quotation from *Sentimental Tommy* by J. M. Barrie, and "Requiem" in *Ballads and Other Poems* by Robert Louis Stevenson.

Finally, I would like to offer my personal thanks to the following people for the comments they made on the manuscript: Professor Marianne Everett Gideon, Temple University; Dr. Edward Hart, Chairperson, Department of Health Education, State University College, Corland, New York; and Dr. Dan Leviton, University of Maryland.

Dale V. Hardt

1

Origins of
Death Attitudes

You want to know of Death?
Well, I shall save my breath.
When you know Life, why then,
We'll talk of Death again.

(CONFUCIUS "Death and Life")

Philosophical, Psychological, Cultural, and Religious Views

What is death? As Confucius suggests, must we know all of life before we can understand death? How do we feel about death? A curious nine-year-old boy asks his mother "Why do people die? Will I die?" His mother responds in a voice that tells him he should not have asked. All too often, people taboo the natural phenomenon of death. It is often too difficult to handle the display of emotion dealing with death; consequently, we avoid it. We mask our fears and discomforts with jokes, fully understanding that we are not going to live forever. In fact, more than 5,250 Americans will die today. Some of us are within minutes of our own deaths. Yet, we ignore and deny it! Current American attitudes toward death are representative of fear and denial. This has not always been the case. Attitudes toward death have undergone radical changes in the last few generations. Rarely will a father, mother, brother, or sister die at home. Furthermore, children will rarely experience the death of loved ones. Their loved ones will die in hospitals and be "taken care of," or they will die away from their homes and loved ones. The natural, inevitable experience of dying will go unnoticed by the dying patient and by family members who could learn and benefit so much from the experience.

We face death most often in newspapers, magazines, or on television programs. Sometimes we get a sob sister approach focusing on the emotional impact. Other times we get a sensationalist or drastic horror approach aimed at such people as drug users and abortionists. In reality, we have become removed from, or desensitized toward, death because it seems only to occur in the papers or on television. Thus, when a loved one dies, we do not know what to say, how to act, or even how to feel. We have not had the time, experience, or education (direct or indirect) that it takes to formulate an attitude toward death. In fact, this process of attitude formation is not as simple as it may seem.

Attitudes toward death comprise a complex area of concern with individual, subcultural, and cultural ramifications. The role of death as a part of the life experience has changed and so have attitudes toward it.

2

Our attitudes are influenced by past experiences with death, family attitudes, religious beliefs, education, maturity, and other such factors. Not only are these attitudes measurable, but just by talking about various aspects of death and dying, attitudes can be improved. In fact, they can be improved to a point where we can understand and accept our own finality as well as the finality of others.

Death is not a taboo subject and it is not meant to be avoided. Our feelings toward death dictate, to some extent, how we will live our lives. If we accept, understand, and talk about death, we will accept life and live it to the fullest. The first step in positive attitude development is the ability to talk about, read, and understand the subject area.

Some Philosophical and Psychological Perspectives On Death. Much of our traditional attitude toward death is derived from previous philosophical, religious, and cultural attitudes, beliefs, and practices. Examination of some of these seems a worthwhile educational endeavor.

Socrates (470-399 B.C.?) believed that no living individual could know death. He offered, however, two possible descriptions for death. He believed death was either a dreamless sleep or a journey of the soul into another world. As the life of Socrates drew to an end, it became apparent that he favored the second option. He referred to death as a freezing and separation of the soul from the body. He suggested that no philosopher is afraid of death, and that a true philosopher actually desires it. Socratic logic followed that since Truth is the main goal of the philosopher and it can only be obtained by the soul, the body is a hindrance in this search for Truth. Furthermore, the body is dependent upon all the senses. These senses manifest themselves through pain or pleasure and can only interfere with the soul's search. Hence, only in death is the soul free of these senses and capable of finding Truth.

We are made aware of Socratic philosophy through the works of Plato (427-347 B.C.?), one of his disciples. Plato was so affected by the trial, imprisonment, and death of Socrates that he wrote four dialogues: *Euthyphro, Apology, Crito,* and *Phaedo.* In *Phaedo* Socrates is living his last day and he discusses death with his friends. Death, as identified by Socrates, holds no terror. He speaks of it as "the fulfillment of his greatest yearning." Plato preaches that death is simply the release of the soul from the body. The soul is not destroyed but achieves immortality. Thus, the mortal body dies while the immortal divine soul, in its desire to be free from fears, passions, and other evils of human existence, proceeds to dwell with the gods. Much of what Plato says regarding death or afterlife was reiterated by Jesus Christ some four hundred years later.

Society differs little today from the society of Plato in its attitudes toward death. Plato suggested that his society refused to recognize death as a process, refused to believe that every person or creature will die, refused to accept that death can be pleasurable, and finally, refused to admit that they need not fear death as evil.

Aristotle (384-322 B.C.), on the other hand, viewed the death of man as the end of everything except his reason. Reason may be identified as something that is learned by every man, is always with him, and hence, does not die.

Later philosophers extended the thoughts of Socrates, Plato, and Aristotle regarding the meaning of death, but it was not until Martin Heidegger that differing philosophies were born. Heidegger, born in 1889, was a German existentialist. His philosophy regarding death is diametrically opposed to that of Socrates and Plato. He believed that death does not separate the soul from the body; rather, it binds them together completing the totality of existence. Death is not an event which ends life, but it is a part of life; therefore, it is always present and does not occur solely at the end of physical existence. Furthermore, death is not something that lies in the future; it is with us here and now. Hence, death permeates all of life. Thus, man must make his own situations while recognizing his mortality. This limits his possibilities by limiting time, and in doing so, gives meaning to life that an eternal being could not experience. Death becomes a goal, rather than a threat, making living more urgent.

Psychologists attempt to explain death through introspection, i.e., examination of thoughts and feelings. By doing so, they may explain and extend the very concepts put forth by these philosophers.

Freud, in explaining the "taboo" nature of death conversation pointed out two distinct types of taboos.

1. The sacred or the consecrated
2. The uncanny, the dangerous, the forbidden and the unclear

Death as a "taboo concept" fits into both of these categories. This explains the reluctance of many to discuss and examine the meaning of death. In fact, Freud wondered if we could really conceptualize our own deaths. His logic supposed that one cannot imagine what one has not yet experienced. Freud concludes by suggesting that in our unconscious we are convinced of our own immortality. Even consciously, it is difficult for us to conceive of our deaths as anything but accidental. Natural death brought about by aging and degeneration is almost unacceptable.

In his later years Freud theorized that every human's actions were directed by series of conflicting instincts. Among them were what he labeled a universal death instinct (Thanatos) and a life principle or instinct (Eros). These two instincts (buried in the Id, that part of the psyche which is completely unconscious) are in opposition throughout the human life. Suicide is seen as a condition that results from the life instinct (desire to live) being overtaken by the death instinct (desire to die). Using these beliefs as his model, Freud maintained that the basis of religion is an attempt by man to lessen his terror of death. In other words, man invented the concepts of soul and afterlife allowing afterlife to be more desirable than earthly existence. By doing this, his fear and lack of understanding regarding death became less frightening.

It must be mentioned that many, if not most, psychologists following Freud rejected his theory on death v. life instincts. Still, it must be admitted that Freud's theory on this matter was, and is, one of the most comprehensive psychological models man has ever constructed in an attempt to find some order within all of the contradictions that surround this phenomenon.

Psychologists, in the years after Freud, often discussed death in terms of *fears* or *terrors*. While Freud suggested that the greatest fear of both men and women is castration (removal of sex glands), Ernest Jones believed that the greatest anxiety results from fear of loss of experiencing pleasure (including sexual pleasure). More recently, Malanie Kleine has suggested that both of these fears, these roots of anxiety, exist, but that the greatest fear of all is the loss of life itself.

Psychologists, philosophers, and even sociologists will continue to explore the concept of death and the fear of death, as well as the rationale behind these fears.

Some Religious and Cultural Perspectives Toward Death. Religious beliefs also play a role in current attitudes and practices regarding the topic of death; these, too, deserve examination.

Interestingly, the Judaic and Christian attitudes toward death are somewhat similar. The question of the resurrection of Jesus Christ constitutes the major difference between the Jewish and Christian faiths. In fact, the whole concept that belief in Jesus Christ is necessary for salvation is offensive to the Jew. Yet, human mortality is maintained in both the Christian Bible and the Hebrew Bible, the Talmud. Both Judaic and Christian traditions believe in resurrection. Differences arise in the interpretation of ideas such as *soul* and *afterlife*. Despite eschatological differences, the attitude the Jew or Christian holds toward death is minimally affected. Just as most attitudes toward death are affected by the thought of our own, so are attitudes influenced by belief or lack of belief in an afterlife. (For the Jew and the Christian, death is the key that opens the doors of eternity.)

Christians believe that the mortal body dies while the soul lives on forever, as Plato had previously suggested. The soul is believed to be whole and unique. It has a free will that is not subject to laws. Since intelligence resides in the soul, the soul controls and directs the body. Therefore, the soul is the essence of life, while the body is just a physical entity. For the true Christian, death is neither a concern nor a fear because faith in the Lord conquers the fear of death. Christians believe that death is a positive element because it is a rest from earthly labor, and it seals union with the Lord. Additionally, death is only absence from the body, and to be absent from the body is to be present with the Lord. A Christian plea that states, "Teach me to live that I may dread the grave as little as my bed" best summarizes the Christian attitude toward death.

A specific Christian sect open to examination of death beliefs and attitudes is the Amish. The Amish movement began in 1693 in Switzerland and was named after Jacob Amman who forced separation from the Mennonite Church. The Amish, after immigrating to the United States, settled in Pennsylvania around 1865 and later moved into Ohio, Indiana, Illinois, Nebraska and some western states. After immigration the Amish order divided into three churches: The Old Order Amish Mennonite Church, The Beachy Amish Mennonite Church, and The Conservative Amish Mennonite Church (that was changed in 1954 to the Conservative Mennonite Conference). Each of the preceding Amish orders varies slightly. The Old Amish Order are still the 'literalists' of the movement in that they cling to their old language and the 17th century culture from which they came. While they object to automobiles, telephones, and higher education, they are recognized as very efficient farmers. The other orders are less disciplined or less restrictive, but they both reflect the image of the Old Order.

Attitudes of the Amish toward death are dissimilar to those of society at large. While death is a sober occasion, it is accepted as a matter of fact. The Amish live in conscious submission to the forces of nature and the will of God. Not only are they content with birth and sickness but with death as well. These religious beliefs are paramount in their lives. Hence, death is not seen as morbid, evil, or taboo. The reasons for death are easily understood within the larger concept of the meaning of life. The Amish reflect on the promise of life after death; therefore, death is not considered the 'greatest menace'.

Islam is the religion of the prophet Mohammed. Worldwide, it claims five hundred million followers, about one-seventh of the human race. In the United States alone, there are an estimated ten-to twenty thousand followers. Islam literally means *absolute submission to God's*

Will. Allah is their God while Mohammed is the messenger of Allah. They do not worship Mohammed; they worship only Allah.

Moslems, those who believe in the religion of Islam, believe in predestination. Thus, the lives and acts of men and the hour of their deaths are preordained by an all-knowing God. They also believe in the existence of angels, the resurrection of man, and reward or punishment in future life that is dependent upon earthly existence. The Koran (the equivalent of the Judeo-Christian Bible) is Allah's truly inspired book.

Moslems believe that on the last day of life, the earth and heavens will quake and man will find himself face to face with Allah. At this time final judgement will be made upon the individual and his good and evil accomplishments in life will be weighed. He will be judged and thereafter enjoy the eternal delights of Heaven (Paradise) or the eternal torments of Hell. Heaven holds the crowning happiness of eternal life where the supreme favor is the direct vision of Allah. Heaven, as identified in the Koran, is a beautiful garden with streams, fruit, rest, shade, and companions. There is neither heat nor cold, but peace, happiness and joy. Hell, on the other hand, has seven gates or means of entrance. It is said that diseased souls suffer in Hell where there is inescapable fire. There are also dry bitter foods, chains, boiling water to drink, and other tortures. However, the greatest torture is that Allah will not speak to or even glance upon these souls.

Some divisions of the Islamic religion have appeared. One such division believes that Heaven and Hell are not eternal places. They believe that all men eventually find admission to Paradise if they suffer the pain and torments of Hell first in payment for their evil earthly deeds.

The beliefs of specific groups, whether religious or cultural in nature, strongly reflect death attitudes. While many beliefs are based on religion, they are generally held by the culture at large regardless of each individual's religiosity.

Almost eighty-five percent of India's inhabitants are Hindu. While Hinduism is a body of customs and beliefs, it is also a way of life. Many Hindu customs and beliefs have religious significance; however, Hinduism is not strictly seen as a religion. The Hindus believe in *karma,* identified as the belief that for every action, there is a good or bad consequence that must be worked out. Thus, Hindus believe that each person's station and lot in life has been determined by his actions in a previous life. Hence, his present life-style and his actions determine his future lives. The Hindu's goal is liberation of the soul through rebirth, i.e., reaching a point in time where the karma represents nothing but good life actions. At this time, the Hindu may be absorbed into Brahma, a state of being that is defined as immaterial, uncreated, limitless, and timeless.

Hindus believe that the outline of their fate is established. However, there is plenty of room for individual choices or decisions. These decisions translate into good and bad deeds that affect the karma. The belief in reincarnation or union with Brahma results in a natural acceptance of death. This is not to say that the Hindu is not sorrowful when death occurs. He merely accepts death as a release of the soul that allows it to continue its cyclical journey. Burial and mourning ceremonies are therefore of the utmost importance in helping the spirit to be purified and eventually reborn.

Chinese attitudes toward death result from a mixing of Buddhism, Confucianism, Taoism, and Shamanism. The Chinese believe in two souls. The first is representative of light, warmth, productivity, and personality. The second, of less importance, is representative of darkness, cold, sterility, and the animal nature. Both souls are believed to leave the body when death occurs.

Chinese belief in reincarnation is much like the Hindus'. Their afterworld is divided into three aspects. The highest and best is called Upper Heaven. The second, or intermediate, is called Western Heaven. The third, or least desirable, is called the Lower Spirit World. If one's life on earth has been virtuous, he may either become a god in the two higher heavens or be reincarnated on earth. If one's life on earth has been bad or wicked, he is either tortured in afterlife or reincarnated as a rat or worm. Hence, the Chinese do not fear death as much as they fear living an evil life. Like the Hindus of India, the more traditional and older Chinese place great emphasis on funerary procedures and ceremonies. These will be examined in a later chapter.

Eskimos inhabit an extensive domain including the arctic coasts of America from Greenland to Alaska and a small part of the adjacent Asiatic coast. Yet, within this vast region, the population is sparce.

Eskimos perceive death differently depending upon their economic and social classes, as well as upon their various geographical residences. Generally, however, Eskimos believe in three sorts of human souls. The first soul, termed the immortal soul, leaves the body at death and proceeds to live in a future world. The second soul is conceptualized as the breath and warmth of the body, and it ceases to exist at death. The third soul is thought to abide in the name of the dead person and is believed to possess traits of the person to whom it relates. Eskimos further believe that upon dying, the immortal soul will continue to be conscious in another world. That world is often conceptualized in terms of earthly existence. Eskimo logic follows that while it may not be a happy place to go, it cannot be filled with any more hardship than their earthly home.

This, compounded by a life-style that forces them to confront death often, results in little fear of death. However, it may be that this fear is only transferred or ritualized, i.e., fear may be present but the Eskimos have learned to deal with it. Thoughts of death by the Eskimo are best described as melancholic.

A specific subgroup of Eskimos, Copper Eskimos, interpret death as a vague and gloomy realm where joy and gladness are unknown. They do not visualize a place of peace where old friends may unite after death, nor do they believe it is a place of misery. Since Eskimo life often seems harder than death, life is often regarded as little to give up. The cultural background of the Eskimo perspective on death is based on the fear of hardships that spirits may cause, in contrast to fear of being punished after they die. (Some interpret this as a transference of their fears to other concerns.)

Copper Eskimos further maintain that death is caused by the malignant activities of such evil spirits. These evil spirits are identified as the 'shade' of the dead or *tarrak*. Consequently, the living use a variety of avoidance measures. They avoid tarrak by avoiding contact with the dying or dead. If contact is made, it is believed that the healthy will become contaminated. In fact, almost all Eskimos avoid the spirit of the dead and dying. These measures include abandoning a house where someone has died, carrying away the body and leaving it alone to die, preparing the body for the grave before death has actually occurred, and discarding all those items that belonged to the dead individual. Some healthy individuals even avoid contact with those who are ill out of fear that the evil spirits or influences may attach themselves to them and cause misfortune. The fear of evil spirits is so great that even illness is attributed to them. If a person becomes ill, a shaman (a priest who uses magic to cure the sick) is called in to diagnose the cause and prescribe a cure. He usually discovers that a taboo has been broken or that the person did something to upset or offend a certain dead person's tarrak. It is not uncommon, in their beliefs, for the tarrak to steal the soul of a living man who then suffers emotionally and dies. They believe that something concrete may be implanted in the body of a healthy person by an offended soul. The shaman must then extract the object with the aid of 'familiar' spirits and implant the illness in or on a physical object that is to be carried away.

In 1922 results of an arctic expedition were published. They relate a story of such a practice. A present consisting of two bone pins fastened to the outside of a deerskin bag was made to one of the explorers involved in the expedition. After leaving the Eskimo settlement, the explorer found four scraps of skin in the bag. It was explained to him by Eskimos in another village that the shaman had placed someone's illness in the bag and added the pins as a 'bribe' to induce the explorer to take it away. Such is the fear that the Eskimo had of the dead.

Some groups of Eskimos have nothing that corresponds to either heaven or hell. They believe that the destination of the soul is dependent upon how the Eskimo died, i.e., natural death, illness, murder, or suicide. Still others believe that the spirit of the dead stays in the house where that person died for four or five days. After that time, it remains near the grave until it enters a newborn child. Ordinarily it will remain until the child dies, but the spirit may be compelled to abandon the child early if the child is habitually punished. These are, to be sure, only a few beliefs of the many different groups of Eskimos regarding death attitudes. As time progresses and other religions and cultures infiltrate the land of the Eskimo, religious beliefs and practices will change. Some of those mentioned in the preceding pages have already changed; however, there are still many Eskimos who maintain traditional beliefs.

American Indian groups also had different beliefs regarding death. The Sioux Indians of Eastern Dakota involved themselves in numerous self-expression or ego preservation activities as a means of overcoming fears, including the fear of death. At death, it was believed that the spirit left the body to travel the 'spirit trail'. Tatoo marks of honor were placed on the wrist, forehead, or chin at death. If absent, the spirit would become a ghost and travel about the earth forever. This indicates that the fear of ghosts was more significant than the fear of death. Again, this may be a case of transference.

Navaho Indians of the Southwest United States believed death was the end to everything good. Like modern American culture, the Navaho Indians believed that death should be avoided for as long as possible. Navahos were also very fearful of ghosts or spirits; they believed that ghosts caused such things as bad dreams, pains, headaches, and weakness in the tribe's members. These fears elicited such practices as never whistling after dark and never stepping across a grave for fear that a ghost might be awakened.

Voodoo is a primitive religion practiced in the West Indies. It is currently explained as power of mind over body. The belief that death can be produced by magical means was unquestionably part of man's early culture. Many such cases have been reported in primitive societies. Although modern man has coined the term "psychophysiological reactions" to cover these phenomena when they occur in his advanced society, actual deaths from such causes are frequently reported.

Rex Burrell, a South African physician, witnessed six cases of middle-aged Bantu men who died after being told, "You will die at sunset." Autopsies failed to show a cause of death. While there was clearly no physiological explanation for these deaths, we can see their psychological precursors. A curse or prophecy predicts death. The victim believes the message, believes he is helpless to do anything about it, becomes passive and depressed, gives up, and dies.

In New Zealand a woman eats fruit that she later learns has come from a taboo place. Her chief has been profaned. By noon of the next day she is dead. In Australia, a witch doctor points a bone at a man. Believing that nothing can save him, the man rapidly sinks in spirit and prepares to die. He is saved only at the last moment when the witch doctor is forced to remove the charm. These individuals believed that they were doomed to die, and that there was nothing they could do to change their fates.

Psychophysiological conditions such as those just mentioned are known to be present in a large percentage of medical patients, but the possibility that emotional factors may contribute in a major way to an illness is not generally considered. Psychological death, whether by weird incantations of a primitive shaman or by the violent wish of a thwarted mother, is a difficult thing for even a scientifically trained physician to accept. Whatever name it is given, it seems evident that such things may occur in a more complex, though less dramatic, form in modern civilization.

SUMMARY

Death thoughts, in our culture, are usually treated as "taboo"; we tend to avoid any mention of death. In this way, we are able to avoid any conscious or subconscious fears we may have concerning the subject. The role that death has played in the total life experience has changed and with the changing role, so have our attitudes. Yet, our attitudes toward death have some effect on how we perceive our lives; and how we perceive our lives has some effect on how we live.

At the root of our death attitudes are past philosophical, religious, cultural, and psychological beliefs. Freud, for example, maintained that the unconscious mind cannot conceive of its own mortality.

Many of our religious beliefs, such as those of Jews, Christians, and Moslems, identify death as the occurrence that precedes eternal life for the soul, the essence of the human.

Other religious beliefs, such as those of the Hindus, view death as that which preceeds another human, physical life on earth. The final goal for the Hindu is freedom of the soul from future lives. Although somewhat different from Hinduism, the Chinese (Buddhists, Confusianists, Taoists, and

Shamanists) also believe in reincarnation. While beliefs of these religions differ, the concept of immortality is in some sense universal.

Life-style also has some effect on attitudes toward death. The life-style of the Eskimo forces him to view death often; hence, fear of death is limited. It is more a part of life than it is in American culture.

Fear of death underlines our entire existence. American Indians, in the past, feared the spirit of the dead more than death itself. Fears surrounding death and dying exemplify the power of the mind. Power of mind over body is best demonstrated by primitive voodoo societies.

SELECTED BIBLIOGRAPHY

BISKET-SMITH, KAJ, *Eskimos.* New York: Crown Publishers, Inc., 1971.

COPLESTON, FREDERICK S. J., *A History of Philosophy, Volume I, Greece and Rome.* Westminister, Maryland: The Newman Press, 1963.

CORNFORD, FRANCIS MACDONALD, *Plato's Cosmology, The Timaeus of Plato.* New York: Bobbs-Merrill Co. Inc., 1937.

CRAGG, KENNETH, *The Event of the Qur'an.* London, England: George Allen and Unwin Ltd., 1971.

DEMOS, RAPHAEL, *Plato, Selections.* Chicago, Illinois: Charles Scribner's Sons, 1927.

DEMSKE, JAMES M., *Being, Man, and Death,* p. 5. Lexington: University Press of Kentucky, 1970.

GARDET, LOUIS, *Mohammedanism.* New York: Hawthorn Books, 1961.

HABENSTEIN, ROBERT W., and WILLIAM M. LAMERS. *Funeral Customs the World Over.* Milwaukee, Wisconsin: Bulfin Printers, Inc., 1960.

HARDT, DALE V., "Investigation of the Improvement of Attitudes Toward Death," *The Journal of School Health,* 46, no. 5 (May 1976) 269–270.

HASSRICK, ROYAL B., *The Sioux.* Norman, Oklahoma: University of Oklahoma Press, 1964.

HOSTETLET, JOHN A., *Amish Society,* pp. 183, 189, Baltimore, Maryland: John Hopkins Press, 1968.

JENNESS, D., "The Life of the Copper Eskimos," *Report of the Canadian Arctic Expedition, 1913–18,* 12 (Ottowa, Canada: F.A. Acland, 1922).

KAPLAN, ABRAHAM, *The New World of Philosophy.* New York: Random House, 1962.

KLEIN, HEIMANN, P., and R. MONEY-DYRLE. *New Directions in Psychoanalysis.* London, England: Tavistock Publications Limited, 1955.

MARA, JOSE FERRATER, *Being and Death.* Berkeley, California: University of California Press, 1965.

MEAD, FRANK S., *Handbook of Denominations in the United States,* pp. 142–46, 162. New York: Abingdon Press, 1965.

STIFF, CARY, "Death—A Subject No One Talks About," *Chicago Today,* Family Today section, January 14, 1974, p. 25, col. 1.

WEYER, EDWARD MOFFAT JR., *The Eskimos: Their Environment and Folkways.* New Haven, Conn.: Yale University Press, 1932.

2

Death:
Attitudes
and Education

Fear death?—to feel the fog in my throat,
    The mist in my face,
When the snows begin, and the blasts denote
    I am nearing the place,
The power of the night, the press of the storm,
    The post of the foe;
Where he stands, the Arch Fear in a visible form,
    Yet the strong man must go:
For the journey is done and the summit attained,
    And the barriers fall,
Though a battle's to fight ere the guerdon be gained,
    The reward of it all.
I was ever a fighter, so—one fight more,
    The best and the last!
I would hate that death bandaged my eyes, and forbore
    And bade me creep past.
No! let me taste the whole of it, fare like my peers
    The heroes of old,
Bear the brunt, in a minute pay glad life's arrears
    Of pain, darkness and cold.
For sudden the worst turns the best to the brave,
    The black minute's at end,
And the elements' rage, the fiend-voices that rave,
    Shall dwindle, shall blend,
Shall change, shall become first a peace out of pain,
    Then a light, then thy breast,
O thou soul of my soul! I shall clasp thee again,
    And with God be the rest!

(ROBERT BROWNING   "Prospice")

American Attitudes Toward Death

While theologians, metaphysicists, and philosophers have given the
topic of death attitudes considerable thought, there have been relatively
few studies dealing with this concern in psychological literature. Because of the nature of the death subject and subsequent fears evoked by
it in American culture, it is not surprising that it is one of our least-
studied subjects.

Psychology Of Death Attitudes. Perhaps the first study concerning
death in general was done by Hall in 1897. Hall gathered reports of
major fears from various sources. While admitting a lack of uniformity in

15

collection methods, he recorded over two thousand reports of these fears, predominantly from adolescents. His total accumulation was nearly four thousand pages long. After breaking the report down by age and sex, he concluded that young children appear to have no instinctive feeling about death. As age increased, so did the number of subjects reporting a fear of death. Hall's study into the realm of attitudes toward death is significant because it is the basic work from which interest in death and death research has commenced.

In 1933, Bromberg and Schilder recorded data concerning the attitudes of 'normal' and neurotic individuals toward death. The authors gave collective impressions of the subjects' attitudes toward death. They concluded that the death attitudes of the mental patients were connected with murder, sado-masochistic trends, punishment by parents, punishment for masturbation, resignation concerning love of parents, fear of castration, escape from reality, self-punishment, and escape from sadistic impulses directed against the father. In the case of 'normal' adults, Bromberg and Schilder found that in the absence of a death experience in childhood, death was simply identified as a mysterious absence that was somehow connected with threats.

Bromberg's and Schilder's study established the conscious and unconscious death thoughts of psychologically abnormal and normal adults. Common attitudes among both groups included:

1. Death as an escape from an unbearable situation
2. Desiring death (a death wish) as a method of forcing others to give more affection
3. Death as the final sexual union in intercourse
4. Death as the final narcissistic perfection (At no other point can you be more in love with yourself.)
5. Death as that which gratifies masochistic tendencies

Bromberg and Schilder concluded from their interpretation of each completed questionnaire that most 'normal' people did not believe in their own deaths. It has been mentioned that Freud had earlier proposed this hypothesis.

Alexander and Adlerstein studied the attitudes and subsequent emotional development of children at various ages toward the concept of death. In this study, reported in 1958, the authors included a word association task and galvanic skin response (GSR). This is one of only two studies that combine attitudinal with physiological stress measurement.

Each subject was studied independently. He was first connected to a machine that measured galvanic skin response. A telephone receiver was placed close to his mouth. Upon hearing a stimulus word from the word list, he was to respond with the first word that came to mind. Recorded were the stimulus word and the change in skin resistance (Galvanic Skin Response).

Analysis of the data revealed that all age groups take significantly longer to respond to death words than to basal words. While the authors concluded that death words generally elicit some indication of increased emotional response, they discussed such results in terms of cultural expectations and ego stability. The most general statement that can be made regarding the results is that death has a greater emotional significance for those who have low self-concepts than it does for those with adequate concepts of themselves.

In another general study, Caprio interviewed 100 males and females of different ages, socioeconomic backgrounds, occupations, educational levels, and religious affiliations. Using the method of free association, each person was asked to recall or relate his or her reaction to the idea of death during prepubertal ages. Particular reference was made to childhood impressions of funerals involving family, friends, or relatives. If you can think back, ask yourself what you thought of death during this period of your life. How did you feel about going to the funeral of a good friend or close relative?

After analyzing the results of his interviews, Caprio concluded the following points:

1. The majority of those interviewed saw death as gloomy, fearful, and/or dark.
2. Neurotic fears in adult life were often the result of childhood attendance at funerals. This does not imply that childhood attendance at funerals is bad. We do not really know the situations. Perhaps the interviewed were forced to go.
3. Anxiety reactions that resulted in an unconscious identification with the dead were found among some of those interviewed.
4. Death was seen as departure to another world. This implies that those interviewed believed in an afterlife.
5. Many neurotic fears in adults can be traced to traumatic experiences involving death scenes in childhood. This is not totally unexpected since psychologists inform us that most of us have neurotic fears anyway.

From the work of Hall, Bromberg and Schilder, and Caprio, it becomes evident that children's views and attitudes regarding death are likely to be different from those of adults. Furthermore, adults tend to begin learning their attitudes toward death during childhood or adolescence. Thus, death attitudes are most likely formed chiefly by childhood experiences. Most of what has just been concluded is assumption. The next logical step is to pursue the attitudinal studies dealing with children and their concepts of death.

With all age groups, the amount of research dealing specifically with death attitudes has not been extensive. The types of investigation concerned with death attitudes of children are similar to death attitude studies of other age groups: questionnaires, written compositions, drawings, discussions, and case studies. All of these lend themselves to a researcher's final interpretation of attitudes toward the concept of death.

In 1934, Schilder and Wechsler studied the death attitudes of children. They concluded that while children can believe in the deaths of others, their own death does not seem probable. In fact, for the majority of children, death consists of deprivation since the dead are deprived of movement. In addition, the death of others is usually linked to some form of violence or is the result of hostility by other people. Children do not conceive of old age or disease as leading to death.

It is interesting to note that the results obtained by Schilder and Wechsler are consistent with research that had been done with other children concerning death attitudes. For example, in 1948 Nagy questioned 378 children between the ages of three and ten concerning the death concept. Nagy found, upon analysis, that there were three stages of development regarding death attitudes. Children from three to five deny death as a regular and final process. Consequently, death is seen as temporary by this age group. Although someone has died, children in this age group believe they will return. Children from five to nine think of death as a person. They perceive death as someone who takes human form, visits those about to die, and takes them away. Children around nine recognize death as a reality, i.e., they know it is inevitable. They realize it is the dissolution of bodily life.

In 1971, Childers and Wimmer tested Nagy's results. Nagy's study supported the hypothesis that a child's perception of death is dependent upon his stage of development or age. Hindsight tells us that it is probably more the stage of development and readiness to learn than it is age; however, for the majority of children the two tend to occur simultaneously.

As in other studies, individual discussions took place with a set of questions being asked of each subject. Childers and Wimmer concluded that children understand death as universal sometime after age nine. While progression in understanding that death is universal increases with the child's age, a cognitive point for understanding that death is irrevocable or irreversible was not established until age ten. Hence, these results support Nagy's. While the ages somewhat differ, the connection between "stage of development" and the death concept are supported.

In summary, we can interpret the results of studies in the area of children's death attitudes as indicating that they do not realistically understand the concept of death as final and irreversible until they are age nine or older. Some children will understand this at a younger age and some at an older age. Regardless, there seems to be agreement in the previous studies that a child's concept of death progresses from a state of nonawareness through a series of intermediate stages to a point where death is understood as logical and natural. Hence, a concrete, realistic knowledge of the concept of death develops around the adolescent years.

In 1954, Stacy and Reichen investigated death and afterlife attitudes of institutional, subnormal adolescent girls and normal adolescent high school girls. Both groups ranged from 14 to 16 years in age. The intelligence level of the subnormal group ranged from IQ 50 to 75. The intelligence level of the normal girls, as measured by various group tests, ranged from average to superior.

Upon analysis of a questionnaire, Stacy and Reichen concluded that there appeared to be sufficient evidence to suggest that there were differences between the attitudes of the two groups toward death and future life. Some of the differences noted were:

The Subnormal Adolescent Girls (Compared to Normal Adolescent Girls)
1. More emotional and fearful of attitudes toward death
2. Think more of dying from a specific fatal disease
3. More horrified by death
4. More depressed by funerals or visiting cemeteries

The Normal Adolescent Girls (Compared to the Subnormal Adolescent Girls)
1. Think of and imagine their own deaths more frequently
2. More often think of being killed in an accident
3. More have attended funerals, visited cemeteries, seen corpses
4. More often think of being buried alive
5. More often wish they were dead

Other results indicated that both groups are similar in that:

1. Both groups dreamed of death. (Dreams of death are not abnormal.)
2. Both groups were not fascinated by death nor did they enjoy reading stories of death. (Do you find stories of death depressing? Again, this is not generally abnormal.)

3. Both groups preferred to have a belief in, rather than a proof of, life after death. (The trend today is toward "proof of" rather than "belief in" afterlife.)

A similar study reported in 1964 by Maurer investigated the attitudes of adolescent girls toward death in relation to academic achievement. Academic achievement was regarded in terms of scholarship as designated by grades. Upon analyzing the results, Maurer concluded that high achievement is associated with a greater sophistication in acknowledging the inevitability of death.

The two previously mentioned studies appear to indicate that educational level or attainment in some way affects one's attitudes toward death. Maurer precisely states that low achievers appear to have more negative attitudes toward the concept of death than do high achievers. This is to be expected since we are aware that knowledge does have some affect on attitudes, and that both of these somehow fit into a rather complex formula leading to behavior.

In 1970, Hogen reported three studies that attempt to demonstrate both adolescent and young-adult attitudes toward death. These people were asked to rank order among seven death-related metaphors. Of their first three choices, differences between the sexes were small. Both male and female subjects preferred to perceive death in terms of "the unknown," "a lost adventure," or "the end of life." Both sexes avoided categories offering threatening sexual or aggressive metaphors such as "Grinning Butcher," "Threatening Father," or "Gay Seducer."

Hogan's second study investigated death-related fantasy experiences. His subjects were told to close their eyes and imagine they were dying of cancer. Cues were presented in order to increase anxiety. They were then told to picture themselves falling asleep, dreaming, and letting the dream drift through their minds. After a few minutes, they were instructed to write down their dreams. The experimenter then analyzed the content of the dreams.

Very few of the subjects had fantasy experiences related to sexual pleasure, but about forty-five percent responded in a manner symbolic of a pleasurable experience such as relaxing outdoors. About thirty-nine percent responded in a manner symbolic of painful experiences like a fear of the unknown or psychological pains like sadness, helplessness, or loneliness. Only about sixteen percent responded in a manner symbolic of indifference. The subcategory most frequently stressed by both sexes related death to a fear of the unknown. This result is consistent with the results of other researchers.

In Hogan's third study, he asked his subjects to write directly about their perceptions and concepts of death. These subjects were not used in the previous two studies. About thirty-eight percent of the cases analyzed related death to a religious experience. Females responded relative to this concept more often than males. About thirty percent of the analyzed cases related death to a biological end. Males responded relative to this concept more often than females. The perception of death most often chosen was, again, fear of the unknown. Hogan's three studies appear to give some basis to the belief that adolescents have realistic attitudes toward death.

Over the years a number of death attitude investigations have been conducted at the college age level. Middleton, in 1937, analyzed the results of a fourteen item questionnaire. Other than sex and age, the questionnaire included items that were relevant to death and life after death. There were no significant differences in the answers given by either sex.

Some of the significant findings of Middleton's study with which you may compare yourself are:

1. About 93% reported that they thought of their own deaths rarely.
2. Approximately 18% reported that they sometimes, (rarely, however), imagined themselves dying or dead.
3. Roughly 21% reported that they sometimes thought of a specific disease which could cause their death. (Perhaps it is interesting that cancer was the most frequently mentioned disease.)
4. About 51% had entertained thoughts regarding death by accident.
5. 8% imagined death as horribly painful.
6. Almost 83% rarely or never wished that they were dead.
7. 16% reported that visiting a cemetery usually depressed them considerably.
8. About 34% reported that they were inclined to be fascinated by newspaper stories of death.
9. Roughly 12% reported that they had a strong fear of death, while 25% reported that they were absolutely unafraid. Interestingly, 62% reported that they have an indifferent attitude toward death.
10. About 78% expressed a strong wish to live after death.
11. 17% reported that the question of future life worried them considerably.

Middleton stated other results in his research, but those mentioned are most relevant to our study. It was his conclusion that most college students show little concern with death.

Then, twenty years later, Alexander, Colby, and Adlerstein attempted to measure simply, directly, physiologically, psychologically, and quantitatively, the affective reactions of male college students to death words. In doing so, they employed a word association task and a psychogalvanic response for recording response time.

Alexander and his associates found that these college students responded to death-related words with greater emotional intensity than to equivalent words drawn from the general language sample. This result indicated that consciously communicated attitudes (spoken) differ from less conscious processes (subconscious) regarding death. In other words, we tend to subconsciously inhibit our verbal attitudes toward death. This indicates a deeper fear of death than was previously expected.

In 1961, Kalish utilized thirty-two attitude items to explore the relationships among variables related to the destruction of life, belief in God and afterlife, and fear of death.

After analyzing the data of his college sample, it was found that of those who approve of abortion, euthanasia, and birth control, the following religious groups appear in order of acceptance: Atheist-Agnostic, Jewish, Protestant, and Catholic (least acceptant). The only difference found between males and females was that men were more acceptant of wartime killing than were women. This is consistent within the concept of sex-role development. However, it is the lack of differences between religious groups in their fear of death that is worth noting.

Kalish continued his work in 1963. In this follow-up study he presented an instrument composed of various demographic data (age, sex, religious affiliation, marital status, race, and frequency of church attendance) and seventy-five Likert-type attitude items. The attitude items were concerned with death, dying, types of life destruction, and religious beliefs.

While age did not significantly correlate with any of the variables, there were some differences among the sexes. However, these appear to relate to traditional roles. Few differences occurred between blacks and whites. While those of Asian ancestry did not approve of the Western concept of a personal god or afterlife, they did believe in the importance of funerals, family attendance at death, and the value of mourning.

Religious differences regarding the variables were evident. The most interesting finding was that regular church goers have less fear and anxiety regarding death and dying than do those who attend irregularly. There are a number of reasons for this finding. Logically, those who believe in God and an afterlife with God fear death minimally. Death brings these people closer to God. Secondly, those who attend church more often are repeatedly confronted with the concept of death. As we have already mentioned, simply talking about and confronting death (even academically) can help us develop more acceptant attitudes toward it.

The studies that relate college-age students and their attitudes toward death appear to be inconsistent. Middleton and Kalish suggest that college-age students show little concern with death. Alexander, Colby, and Adlerstein suggest that college students are concerned with death but subconsciously inhibit their real attitudes toward it. Additionally, Kalish indicates that while differences were not found between religious groups, they were found between regular church goers and irregular church goers, with regular church goers having less fear and anxiety regarding death.

As you can see, the research done to date has been minimal but meaningful. It has raised more questions than it has answered, but at least we can begin to understand our own attitudes by looking at those of others. More important, we can understand the stages of attitudinal development.

Children and Death Education

My fairest child, I have no song to
  give you;
No lark could pipe to skies so dull
  and gray;
Yet, ere we part, one lesson I can
  leave you
For every day:
Be good, sweet maid, and let who will
  be clever;
Do noble things, not dream them,
  all day long;
And so make life, death, and that vast
  Forever
One grand, sweet song.

(CHARLES KINGSLEY "A Farewell")

From the preceding studies, it can be summarized that a child goes through stages of understanding the concept of death until, around age nine, he finally grasps its reality. As an infant, his world is composed only of his personal needs. As a toddler, the world appears to revolve around him, his desires, and his wishes. By preschool age, the child has probably been exposed to death by way of pet, relative, or media. By school-age, his concept of death begins to develop. As we saw earlier in this chapter, the development of a mature, realistic concept of death is a rather slow process that parallels the development of our self-concept.

Traditionally, parents, adults, and even teachers try to keep any ideas on the subject away from children. This is most likely a direct result of their own fears regarding the finality of death. But all that silence does little good; death does not stand still. We are surrounded by it. Fairy tales such as Hansel and Gretel, the Witch Killers, or Sleeping Beauty are told to children at bedtime. The prayers they learn ("Now I lay me down to sleep... If I should die before I wake") refer to death. Movies portray death as the great depriver, and, usually, as a temporary state of being. (This week's villain in a tv series is in next week's movie.) Yes, death is all around us. It is a subject that cannot be avoided. Children have questions that must be answered: "What is death?" "What makes people die?" "What happens to people, and where do they go when they die?" Hence, while a young child may not comprehend death, death themes appear early in his life. These themes inevitably bring with them questions. These questions must be answered honestly and on the child's level because death will not go away if we ignore it.

But what if a child experiences the death of a loved one? What do we say? There are experiences and attitudes that should be encouraged. You can begin by telling the child about the death. Depending on your perspective, you can proceed in one of two ways. From a religious approach, you can utilize the following capsular logic: "There is God; God is loving; God's love is greater than all human existence; God can be trusted; your loved one is now with God." Or perhaps you can utilize a factual, scientific approach: "When death occurs, life stops and the dead cannot return. They are buried and become part of the earth." Of course, each of the examples can be altered; however, the basic premise is that you are honest with the child. In being honest with the child, you must have come to terms with the death concept yourself. Otherwise, you may do nothing but reflect your own fears.

Second, you should explain the cause of death to eliminate any possible fear or anxiety the child may develop. It is therefore not recommended that one deceive the child. In telling a child that death is a long sleep one can do more harm than good. It is very important to explain the difference between sleep and death. Young children may lie awake all night for fear of going to "eternal sleep," never again to awaken. Telling a child that "Grandpa is on a long trip" or "Mother is visiting friends a long way from here" is also bad. Children have ways of knowing when you, a parent, are not telling the truth. Anxiety will build if a child feels something is being hidden from him. Since young children are egocentric and possess almost primitive beliefs in magic, they must be told that they had no part in causing the death. Otherwise, anxiety may build to a fear of causation. Deception concerning death causation could do much to eliminate the mutual trust that most parents strive for with their children.

Third, you should encourage the child to talk about his fears and feelings. You can do this only if you maintain an open atmosphere, one of empathy, love, and understanding. Allow him to express his feelings as he remembers his experiences with the deceased. The child has a strong need to talk, he does not need a talking-to. Overexplanation can also become too complicated and confusing. Listen; however, do not attach adult meanings to his expressions. Do not criticize him for what he thinks just because it does not agree with your own analysis. Grief demands expression! Thus, the child should not be discouraged from crying because tears are the first and most natural tribute that can be paid to one who is gone. Parents often avoid letting the child cry because *they* fear the tears that may follow. To inhibit the crying process may inhibit the mourning process. This is especially true with male children who are often told: "Don't cry," "Men don't cry," or "Be a man." Obviously, parents fail to understand that crying is a natural reaction; hence, it is a natural way of showing grief. However, just as parents should not inhibit the crying process, neither should they encourage him to display unfelt sorrow. Parents often believe that because they were close to Uncle Willie, so was their child. This may not be the case.

Fourth, you should prepare the child for the funeral. Funerals enable the child to accept the reality of death. Many parents feel funerals are too sad and traumatic for a small child to attend. Yet recognized child authorities have come to the conclusion that not only is it correct to permit a child to attend a funeral, but from approximately the age of seven, a child should be encouraged to attend. This does not mean the child should be forced to go if he does not want to. Similarily, the child should be encouraged to participate in funeral services or scripture readings. Doing so will aid in his future acceptance of the death concept. To exclude the child from these experiences leaves him with what few facts he may have. These facts plus his imagination may cause him to construct an inaccurate analysis of the event. The result of this may not show up until much later in life.

Last, the child should be allowed to mourn. Mourning is a valuable expression of grief. It is a healing process that helps the child to face and to recover from the loss. Overall, you should show the child the courage and acceptance of death that it takes to continue life. You should be aware that the child may model his future behavior after your example.

It is also important for you to understand that not all children will accept death when it happens to a loved one. They may deny the fact that death has occurred. This conscious denial may precipitate nightmares in adults as well as in children. Children may even display signs of hostility toward the deceased by saying such things as, "How could you do this to me?" They may also show hostility toward others or perhaps show guilt. All of these, if temporary, are normal reactions of children to death. If they appear to be permanent, guidance should be sought.

But Why Death Education? Let us face the issue. The place for sex education and death education, as they are called, is the home. Both are fundamental parental responsibilities. So why should the school get involved? Simply because many parents are failing to perform their responsibilities. For whatever reason (fear, ignorance, embarrassment) most parents do not want the job of educating their children in such matters. In school, education is supposed to prepare children for life. Should education also prepare them to handle concerns related to death? The answer to this question appears to be an emphatic 'yes'. Summarizing a concern from the first chapter, in earlier days both birth and death occurred in the home. Children were more than familiar with birth and death. Today, the majority of Americans are born and die in hospitals. These experiences are removed from the home, hence, removed from the child. Thus, when children meet death or start asking about it, they depend upon parents and teachers to help guide them toward intellectual understanding, support, and empathy. Even if an emotional crisis has not arisen, we can help children understand death by talking about it as it is, a natural and everyday experience.

Eliot, Leviton, Hair, and Symes are in general agreement that attitudes toward and knowledge about death are as important as attitudes toward and knowledge about sex. It is quite obvious that matters such as death and suicide, like sexuality, are being recognized as areas closely related to the ability to live happily. The overall concept is not one that is suddenly taught at age nine or grade five; rather, it should be a gradual and continuous process that extends throughout the child's life.

Although attitudes are learned, they can be changed through the normal life processes of thinking, inhibition, extinction, and fatigue. As such, attitudes can change over a period of time. Hence, children need some form of education regarding death to help them form a favorable attitude concerning death. Additionally, most of us agree that a child should learn to accept death as a natural process of life and as part of his existence. Where is he going to learn these things if parents do not do the teaching? The obvious answer is in school.

Research in prominent journals suggested death education as early as 1933. While some of the earlier articles suggested it as a function of parents (Lillian Symes), later articles suggested that it be a function of the schools. Brubacher, just before World War II, saw the need to emotionally prepare high school boys for war and the possibility of death.

Literature supporting death education in the schools became rather scarce from the end of World War II until the middle and later 1960s. It was then that the current death education movement began. Realizing that children may be unable to meet an emotional crisis such as the death of a parent, and noting that the end of living was perhaps the most neglected area of study within the whole life cycle, article after article was written suggesting the school offer help toward this concern. Such people as Arthur and Kemme, Hair, Plank, Leviton, and Kubler-Ross have supported the death education movement. They have led the way in demonstrating the need for such education.

Apparently, educators have picked up the additional task of including death education in their curriculums. As of 1975 Dr. Austin Kutscher, President of the Foundation of Thanatology, suggested that more than one thousand high schools and four hundred colleges offer credit courses.

Whether or not educators choose to include death education in their curriculums partially depends on prevailing attitudes toward death because attitudes play a significant role in learning and understanding. The study of death attitudes is significant not only for research concerns, but it should serve as a basis on which to plan a death education unit. If such a unit is deemed necessary, it should reflect attitudes toward death and should enable educators to remove another road block in the development of emotional and social attitudes. This would surely remove the stigma, mythology, and fear that surrounds the death concept and would enable us to understand ourselves more fully.

SUMMARY

Past psychological studies of attitudes toward death demonstrate a number of important foundations regarding our ability to understand death.

Since young children do not demonstrate an instinctive feeling regarding death, it becomes apparent that death attitudes are learned, i.e., they are the end products of the socialization process.* Furthermore, conceptualization of death occurs in progressive stages beginning around age three. From about three to five years old, death appears to be a rather temporary process. Children from about five to nine years old perceive death as a person, someone who comes and takes his loved ones away. Finally, somewhere around age nine, a child is able to conceptualize death. He is able to understand death as an inevitable, final reality. The process does not stop here but continues to mature with the individual. Now

---

*Note: I realize this contradicts Freud's *thanatos* but, as mentioned before, the concept of *Thanatos* v. *Eros* has been discounted by most psychologists.

fears that are learned enter the picture. The adolescent typically describes death in terms of fear of the unknown. Intelligence, religion, sex, and social status are all in some way related to an adolescent's attitude toward death. Exactly how each affects such an attitude is not precisely known.

College students tend to demonstrate very little concern with death. Yet if Freud is correct, perhaps they subconsciously inhibit their real attitudes. As the individual matures, it becomes apparent that those with adequate self-concepts are not as emotionally disturbed by death and dying as are people with in-adequate self-concepts.

Children's questions on death need to be answered honestly and precisely. Death is not something that can be avoided. It is present everyday of our lives in the media. Schools have increasingly accepted their role in death education because of parental reluctance or inability to discuss this concept. However negative prevailing attitudes are, appropriate education programs can change these attitudes toward a more positive end.

SELECTED BIBLIOGRAPHY

ALEXANDER, IRVING AND ARTHUR ADLERSTEIN, "Affective Responses to the Concept of Death in a Population of Children and Early Adolescents," *The Journal of Genetic Psychology,* 93 (December 1958), 167–177.

ALEXANDER, IRVING, RANDOLPH COLLEY, AND ARTHUR ADLERSTEIN, "Is Death a Matter of Indifference," *The Journal of Psychology,* 43 (April 1957), 277–283.

ANTHONY, SYLVIA, *The Child's Discovery of Death,* p. 178. New York: Harcourt Brace, 1940.

ARTHUR, BETTIE AND MARY KEMME, "Bereavement in Childhood," *Journal of Child Psychology and Psychiatry,* 5 (December 1964), 37.

BROMBERG, WALTER AND PAUL SCHILDER, "The Attitude of Psychoneurotics Towards Death," *The Psychoanalytic Review,* 23, no. 1 (January 1936), 2.

BRUBACHER, JOHN, "Education for Death," *School and Society,* 56, no. 1443 (August 1942) 137.

CAPRIO, FRANK, "A Study of Some Psychological Reactions During Pre-Pubescence to the Idea of Death," *Psychiatric Quarterly,* 24 (January 1950), 495–505.

CHILDERS, PAUL AND MARY WIMMER, "The Concept of Death in Early Childhood," *Child Development*, 42, no. 4 (October 1971), 1299–1301.

"Children View Death in Many Ways," *Science Digest*, 73, no. 5 (May 1973), 88–89.

DARCY-BERUBE, FRANCOISE, "When Your Child Asks about Death," *New Catholic World*, 216, no. 1289 (March 1973), 55–57.

ELIOT, THOMAS, "A Step Toward the Social Psychology of Bereavement," *Journal of Abnormal and Social Psychology*, 27, no. 4 (January 1933), 380–381.

GIBNEY, HARRIET, "What Death Means to Children," *Parents Magazine*, 40, no. 3 (March 1965), 64–65.

GROLLMAN, EARL, *Explaining Death to Children*. Boston: Beacon Press, 1967.

HAIR, JEANNE, "What Shall We Teach about Death in Science Classes?" *The Elementary School Journal*, 65, no. 8 (May 1965), 414.

HALL, STANLEY, "A Study of Fears," *The American Journal of Psychology*, 8, no. 2 (January 1897), 147–224.

HOGAN, ROBERT, "Adolescent Views of Death," *Adolescence*, 5, no. 17 (Spring 1970), 55–66.

JACKSON, PAT LUDDER, "The Child's Developing Concept of Death," *Nursing Forum*, 14, no. 2 (1975), 204.

KALISH, RICHARD, "An Approach to the Study of Death Attitudes," *The American Behavioral Scientist*, 6, no. 9 (May 1963), 68–70.

KALISH, R. A. "Some Variables in Death Attitudes," *The Journal of Social Psychology*, 59 (February 1963), 137–145.

KASTENBAUM, ROBERT, "Kingdom Where Nobody Dies," *Saturday Review*, 23 (December 23, 1972), 33–38.

KOSTER, JOHN, "Death Rap Lasts All Night Long," *The Sunday Record* (Bergen County, N.J.), March 16, 1975.

KUBLER-ROSS, ELISABETH, "The Searching Mind," *Today's Education*, 61, no. 1 (January 1972), 32.

LEVIN, PHYLLIS, "Breaking the News of Death," *New York Times Magazine*, February 21, 1965, p. 47.

LEVITON, DAN, "Education for Death," *Journal of Health, Physical Education, and Recreation*, 40, no. 7 (September 1969), 46–47.

Leviton, Dan, "The Need for Education on Death and Suicide," *The Journal of School Health*, 39, no. 4 (April 1969), 270.

Martin, Mildred Crowl, "Helping Children Cope With Sorrow," *Parents Magazine*, 45, no. 8 (August 1970),

Maurer, Adah, "Adolescent Attitudes Toward Death," *The Journal of Genetic Psychology*, 105 (September 1964), 75–90.

Middleton, Warren, "Some Reactions Toward Death Among College Students," *Journal of Abnormal and Social Psychology*, 31, no. 2 (July 1937), 165–173.

Nagy, Maria, "The Child's Theory Concerning Death," *The Journal of Genetic Psychology*, 73 (September 1948), 3–27.

Piaget, Jean, *The Language and Thought of the Child*, p. 178. London: Routledge, 1959.

Plank, Emma, "Young Children and Death," *Young Children*, 23, no. 6 (September 1968), pp. 331–36.

Ramos, Suzanne, "Hardest Lesson of All: Learning about Death," *New York Times Magazine*, December 10, 1972, pp. 94–95.

Reed, Elizabeth L., *Helping Children With the Mystery of Death*. Nashville and New York: Abingdon Press, 1970.

Schilder, Paul and David Wechsler, "The Attitudes of Children Toward Death," *The Journal of Genetic Psychology*, 45 (September 1934), 406–51.

Shaw, Marvin and Jack Wright, *Scales for the Measurement of Attitudes*, p. 8. New York: McGraw-Hill Book Company, 1967.

Stacy, Chalmer and Marie Reichen, "Attitudes Toward Death and Future Life," *Exceptional Children*, 20, no. 1 (March 1954), 259–62.

Symes, Lillian, "Death and the Child," *Child Study*, 10 (February 1933), 139.

Voiorst, Jane, "Let Us Talk about Death," *Redbook*, 141, no. 2 (June 1973), 33–34.

3

Death: A Flat EEG?

The song of Kilvani: fairest she
In all the land of Savatthi.
She had one child, as sweet and gay
And dear to her as the light of day.
She was so young, and he so fair,
The same bright eyes and the same dark hair;
To see them by the blossomy way,
They seemed two children at their play.

There came a death-dart from the sky,
Kilvani saw her darling die.
The glimmering shade his eyes invades,
Out of his cheek the red bloom fades,
His warm heart feels the icy chill,
The round limbs shudder, and are still.
And yet Kilvani held him fast
Long after life's last pulse was past,
As if her kisses could restore
The smile gone out forevermore.

(JOHN HAY   "The Law of Death")

From Premature Burial to a Definition of Death

How simple death used to be. Night was night, day was day, and death
was death, right? Wrong! If one reviews journals and newspapers from
the turn of the century, it becomes apparent that definitive characteristics of death were avoided by medical personnel. This was not true of a
large number of writers and concerned citizens though, and for good
reason. Numerous occurrences of premature burial occurred around
that time period.

In 1877, the *British Medical Journal* reported the following:

A correspondent at Naples states that the Appeals Court has had before it
a case not likely to inspire confidence in the minds of those who look
forward with horror to the possibility of being buried alive. It appeared
from the evidence that some time ago, a woman was interred with all the
usual formalities, it being believed that she was dead, while she was only in
a trance. Some days afterwards, when the grave in which she had been
placed was opened for the reception of another body, it was found that the
clothes which covered the unfortunate woman were torn to pieces, and that
she had even broken her limbs in attempting to extricate herself from the

living tomb. The Court, after hearing the case, sentenced the doctor who had signed the certificate of decease, and the Major who had authorized the interment each to three month's imprisonment for involuntary manslaughter.[1]

In 1887, *Lancet* reported two separate cases of premature burial.

In the first case a young man afflicted with a contagious disease died suddenly. His body was enshrouded and encoffined, but as the undertaker's men were carrying "the remains" to their last resting place, they heard what was believed to be a knocking against the coffin lid. This sound was repeated in the grave. Instead of testing the evidence of their senses, the men, in accordance with judicial custom, sent for the Mayor, in whose presence the lid was removed from the coffin. Whereupon, to the horror of the spectators, it was observed that the dead man had only just succumbed to asphyxia. In the second case of apparent death, an inhabitant of Mount Joy, Paramatta, was believed to be dead. His supposed remains were about to be committed, when a mourning relative startled the bystanders by exclaiming, "I must see my father once more; something tells me he is not dead!" The coffin was thereupon opened and found to contain a living inmate, who justified the presentiment of his son by slowly recovering.[2]

In 1896, the Fort Randall Cemetery had to be moved. T. M. Montgomery reported the following:

We found among these remains, two that bore every evidence of having been buried alive. The first case was that of a soldier that (sic) had been struck by lightning. Upon opening the lid of the coffin, we found that the legs and arms had been drawn up as far as the confines of the coffin would permit. The other was a case of death resulting from alcoholism. The body was slightly turned, the legs were drawn up a trifle and the hands were clutching the clothing. In the coffin was found a large whiskey flask. Nearly 2 percent of those exhumed here were no doubt victims of suspended animation.[3]

Dr. Franz Hartmann, in his book *Premature Burial* tells the story of a postmaster in a village called Moravia who had apparently died. About a year after his death, a portion of the bodies in the graveyard in which he was buried had to be moved to make room for enlarging the church. His body was one of those. As it was removed, it became evident that he had been buried alive. As a result of this, the physician who had signed the death certificate went insane.

As we have seen, fear of premature burial during those years was a matter to be dealt with. Some physicians attempted to develop methods that would aid in the diagnosis of death "beyond any doubt." One such method is discussed in *Current Literature* in 1907.

> Another "infallible" proof of death—now shown to be untrustworthy—is obtained by means of the diaphanous test. This test consists in holding in front of and close to a strong artificial light the hand of the person believed to be dead, the fingers being extended and just touching one another. The theory is that if the line of scarlet runs around the finger the body is still alive, but that if it is no longer visible, death has actually taken place. So strongly impressed with the value of this discovery was the French Academy of Medicine, that it promised to reward the discoverer very handsomely. Yet Sir Benjamin W. Richardson, after testing it with great care, pronounced it to be a test of only secondary importance. Dr. Edwin Haward proved it to be not infallible. Dr. Gannal maintains that 'the loss of transparency of the fingers is an uncertain sign, because with certain subjects it takes place some time before death; next because it does not always occur in a corpse, and finally, because it exists under certain circumstances in sick persons." Dr. Orfila says the sign is valueless.[4]

Rigor mortis was supposed to be another positive proof of death. This indication was denounced by Dr. Samuel Barker Pratt, an authority of that time. Still other physicians refused to confront the issue because they did not want people to believe that they could not distinguish between life and death. They felt that if this were the case, their patients might lose confidence in them.

Meanwhile, others declared that decomposition was the only reliable sign of death. Dr. Franz Hartmann believed that the certificate of a doctor or an undertaker should give no assurance that death had taken place. The only reliable sign of it, he maintained, was the decomposition of the vital organs. The German nation was so strongly affected by the fear of premature burials that they established "waiting mortuaries" in many of their cities as early as 1823. Described in part, a "waiting mortuary" had a caretaker always on duty and included ...

> ...a narrow cell containing the bell apparatus, which is enclosed in a long cupboard. Windows look out into the mortuary. It is here that the caretaker passes the greater part of his existence. In the evening, he stretches out on his couch where the slightest tinkle of the bell will arouse him. This happens frequently, the warning bell is so sensitive that the slightest shake of the corpse sets it in motion. Various causes may agitate the bell but the waking of a corpse is a rare occurrence.[5]

As previously suggested, fear regarding apparent death and premature burial was well founded. In fact, it is reported that around 1907,

Lady Burton told Mr. Tozer (who had collected a mass of evidence indicative of hastily written death certificates) that some thirty forms of diseases or disorders can produce all the usual symptoms of death. Such diseases or disorders include trance, catalepsy, hysteria, chorea, hypnotism, somnambulism and neurasthenia, conditions produced by a stroke of lightning, sunstroke and anesthesia from chloroform, eclamptic soma in pregnancy, stillbirth, asphyxia from various gases, vapors, smoke, narcotism from opium and other agents, convulsive maladies, drowning, nervous shock from gunshot or electricity, smothering under snow, strangulation, epilepsy, mental and physical exhaustion, syncope, extreme heat and cold, alcoholic intoxication, hemorrhages, suspended animation from mental disorders, excessive emotion, fright, intense excitement, apoplectic seizures, and so-called heart failures.

Around the same time period, Dr. Franz Hartmann had collected some seven hundred cases of premature burial or narrow escapes from it. Mr. James R. Williamson, a promoter of The Society for the Prevention of Premature Burial (an association founded in 1896) is reported to have declared that he "could fill a volume" with descriptions of similar cases. So great was the fear of being buried alive that well-known figures of the time, including Edmund Yates and Hans Christian Anderson, left instructions in their wills regarding techniques to be carried out upon their deaths.

Embalming might appear to answer the problem of premature burial in modern society, but even today the United States is one of the few countries to employ embalming as a preburial technique. Since, however, embalming is generally practiced in the United States, fear of premature burial in this country should be alleviated. Still, a few cases have occurred where a patient has awakened on the embalmer's table after having been declared dead.

While mortuary science students are encouraged to look for signs of life (and many do), this is not required of them. It is usually assumed that death has been determined and that a death certificate will be sent within a few days. This assumption is "most often" correct!

Coverage of the fear of premature burial would not be complete without a discussion of a life-signal device. Arnold, Zimmerman, and Martin, in their paper entitled "Public Attitudes and the Diagnosis of Death," include a translated explanation of such a device patented in Berlin in 1897. The device is described as a

... long tube three and one-half inches in diameter, and a hermetically sealed box. The box is fixed in an aperture in the coffin as soon as the latter is lowered in the grave. No gases can escape from the tomb into the outside air, as the metallic box into which the upper end of the tube enters cannot be opened from the outside. On the chest of the supposed dead body is placed a glass ball which communicates through the tube with an iron box above ground. At the slightest movement of the chest wall, such as breathing or body movement, the glass bell releases a spring which opens the box immediately, thus admitting light and air to the coffin. At the same time, a flag rises perpendicularly about four feet above the ground, and a bell is set ringing which continues for about half an hour. In front of the box is a lamp which gives light after sunset to the coffin below. The tube also acts as a speaking tube which amplifies the voice of the inmate of the coffin, however feeble.[6]

Today, we have added the electrocardiogram and the electroencephalogram as tools for diagnosing death. Interestingly, authorities in the area suggest that they are not often used today in the diagnosis of death.

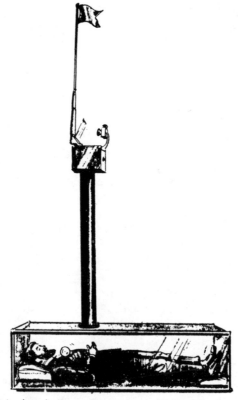

A glass bell on the corpse's chest released a spring if there was movement in the coffin. This opened the lid, rang a bell and raised a flag.

As few as twenty-five years ago, a patient might have been hooked up to an electrocardiogram to make sure death had occurred. Or, he may have been injected with epinephrine, a heart stimulant, which might produce a few more heartbeats, but after that, if the heart stopped, he was dead. Death was identified as a point in time.

With increased concern over the use of donors in single organ transplants (which results in death of the donor if it has not already occurred) and the use of life support systems, the time of death has been the focal point of many committees and subcommittees. There have been numerous attempts to redefine death or to diagnose it more accurately. Part of the problem in redefining death surrounds the current belief that death is *NOT* a point in time; rather, it is a process. It is generally considered that there is a "point" of irreversibility during this process that doctors are able to diagnose. However, because of the great number of considerations involved in the diagnosis of this point, diagnoses may differ among doctors. Hence, the problem of definition still exists.

Traditionally, physicians describe three phases during which different parts of the body die. The first is Clinical Death during which the heart ceases to beat and respiration halts. The second phase is Brain Death resulting from insufficient oxygen to the brain. Finally, Cellular Death occurs; during this time the different cells of the body die at different rates. Unfortunately, for purposes of definition, the first two phases can occur in reverse order. Adding to the confusion are the medical-technological advances that now make it possible to maintain the function of the heart and lungs by artificial means over extended periods of time. It has occurred in a particular case that nondefinitional considerations such as "intuition" on the part of doctors have given them hope of life for a patient, a patient who was only alive because of the machines he was hooked up to. After weeks, a flat EEG (no brain waves) began to suddenly show new brain activity. The patient recovered and lived a normal life in excellent physical *and* mental condition. With a different doctor, this patient may have been declared dead and unhooked from the life-saving machines. This indicates that intuition should perhaps remain an additional indication of death.

In 1968, the council of the International Organization of Medical Science established five criteria leading to a diagnosis of death. Summarized, they are:

1. Loss of all response to the environment
2. Complete abolition of reflexes and loss of muscle tone
3. Cessation of spontaneous respiration
4. Abrupt decline in arterial blood pressure

5. A flat EEG (Electroencephalogram indicating lack of brain activity)

If these five criteria were applied in the "intuitive" case previously mentioned, perhaps that patient would have been taken off the machines and left to die. Obviously, these criteria were insufficient.

An extension of these criteria involving brain death has been suggested. Dr. Julius Korein proposes that Cerebral Death should be the determinant of death. He distinguishes between Brain Death and Cerebral Death indicating that Brain Death includes death of the entire brain including the brain stem while Cerebral Death is only a part of Brain Death. In fact, the brain itself dies in stages. The first part of the brain to die from lack of oxygen is the cerebral cortex. It is this portion of the brain in which higher thought processes occur (these include the decision-making and memory functions). Second, the midbrain dies, and finally, the brain stem ceases to function. If the cerebral cortex dies but the midbrain and brain stem are still alive, the victim will be unconscious. However, the functions of the heart and lungs may continue for an extended period of time without mechanical support. The following excerpt from an article of a local newspaper demonstrates this concept:

> Timothy Turney, 14, in a coma for nine years, has died. He was only five when struck by a hit-run driver Jan. 27, 1967, near his East Oakland home. Timothy had known nothing since he was struck, doctors said. He suffered a severe injury to the brain stem and never recovered consciousness. They said he continued to breathe on his own and was not kept alive by machines. The Alameda County Coroner's office reported that Timothy died Sunday at Fairmont Hospital.[7]

Cerebral Death, as suggested, is obviously the first stage of total brain death. Assuming heart and respiratory functions were present (with or without mechanical help), this would still allow the transplantation of viable organs.

Whatever the definition, a question of morality is quite evident. Should the definition be tied to the concept of organ transplants? Should the definition be tied to the patient, i.e., is he dead beyond any doubt? Or, should continued attempts be made to define death in favor of both concerns whenever possible? Legal cases are becoming more and more prevalent regarding the definition of death. On March 7, 1975 a few physicians at Jacobi Hospital in the Bronx transplanted the kidneys of a slain man into two waiting recipients. This was done in defiance of the city's acting Chief Medical Examiner, who is responsible for determining the cause of death. His position stated that autopsies be performed on all homicide cases prior to the use of the deceased's organs. The physicians argued that such an autopsy takes time and so the organs may deteriorate beyond a point where they are usable. Many were hoping that this case would result in a legal definition of death. However, lawyers for both sides negotiated an agreement on future policy. The doctors noted that numerous transplants could not be made in the past because of objections from the acting Chief Medical Examiner.

As you can see, legal cases arise, but few offer solutions regarding a definition of death. Many authorities suggest that we attempt to find that point at which time the brain is completely dead, yet organs are still transplantable. Still others suggest that such a definition is unnecessary and could actually lead to a surplus of organs, hence, a waste of organs that cannot be stored. Of course we must wonder if it would not be better to have a surplus rather than a deficit of such organs.

The general "rule" followed at the present time is that death is declared when the brain ceases to function (a flat EEG), regardless of breathing and respiration maintained by artificial means. This not only allows the physician to transplant organs but is financially reasonable for the family. Estimated costs for continuation of "life" for a patient such as the one described above exceed one thousand dollars a day. While it is extremely difficult to place a dollar value on life, it is a concern that must be considered.

Still, new task forces are organized to discuss the definition of death. Most of them have offered additional concerns and additional elements to take into consideration. Others have clarified existing definitions. There are probably no more acceptable guidelines than those set up by a Harvard University Committee composed of scholars from various disciplines. Briefly, the four concerns describing death are:

1. Unreceptivity and Unresponsiveness: basically, total unawareness of external stimuli and complete unresponsiveness
2. No movements or breathing: observable by physicians for at least one hour
3. No reflexes: central nervous system activity absent
4. Flat EEG: no brain activity

Additionally, these criteria should be monitored for a minimum of twenty-four hours by competent medical personnel. After the twenty-four hour period, the patient may be considered dead. Exceptions to the above exist, including individuals suffering from overdoses of CNS (central nervous system) depressants. These criteria have been applied to actual patients and have been proven valid and reliable criteria for defining death.

The basic components of the Harvard guidelines include the previous concerns of cessation of respiratory and circulatory functions and brain wave death. Additionally, it includes the complete failure of the functions of the nervous system. Since in most cases the patient is sustained by machines, transplantation is possible after this twenty-four hour period.

It is perhaps worthy to note that the law has done little to resolve the definitional crisis surrounding the 'time' of death. Perhaps this is for the best. Some states have experienced difficulty with a written, legally binding definition of death. For instance, when can a physician turn off a respirator or a heart-lung machine? In most states, it is the absence of a law defining death that gives the physician the freedom to legally determine when death has occurred. While some physicians do not wish to make that legal and moral decision, many authorities agree that it is their responsibility. In December of 1973 the House of Delegates of the American Medical Association met in Anaheim, California. They adopted the following recommendations:

1. ...that, at the present, statutory definition of death is neither desirable or necessary,
2. ...that state medical associations urge their respective legislature to postpone enactment of legislation defining death by statute, and
3. ...that this House of Delegates affirm: Death shall be determined by the clinical judgement of the physician using the necessary available and currently accepted criteria.[8]

Such is the position of the AMA on the definition of death. Obviously, 'currently accepted criteria' refers to those previously mentioned as discussed by the Harvard University Committee. It is hoped that continuing efforts will be made regarding medical clarification of this and future definitions. Such constant concern not only protects future patients against premature assaults in the name of transplanting, but it also protects future patients against extraordinary measures to maintain life at all costs in the name of medicine and the Hippocratic Oath. We must remember that while medicine can often prolong life, in doing so, it may also prolong suffering.

Transplants

The Gods they robbed me of my life, and turned me into stone.
Praxiteles made marble breathe, and gave me back my own.

(ANONYMOUS - "On A Niobe of Praxiteles" TRANSLATED BY GEORGE B. GRUNDY)

Transplantation refers to the grafting of tissues from one part of the body to another part or to that of another body. Historically, accounts of tissue grafting date back to the early Hindus. Six hundred years before the birth of Christ, Hindu surgeons reconstructed noses from skin taken from the arm. Although the surgical procedures were crude, they were reportedly successful.

Today medical science is capable of transplanting nearly twenty-five different tissues and organs. Such structural tissues as bone, tendon (that which attaches muscle to bone), heart valves, fascia (the tissue that covers muscles), the membrane covering the brain, and cartilage can be stored for extended periods of time in tissue banks. Other types of tissues and organs that can be transplanted are corneas (the clear portion in the front of the eye), blood vessels, kidneys, hearts, livers, lungs, pancreases, even bone marrow. Some are quite successful while others are still classified as research.

To understand the basis of transplantation, it is necessary to recognize the four types of grafting being used and experimented with today.

1. Autografts: A skin graft removed from one part of the body and transplanted to another site in the same individual. Autografts are not prone to rejection; a term used to explain the internal body chemistry that enables the body to dispose of, or throw off, a foreign body.
2. Isografts: Grafts between identical twins or highly inbred animals. Isografts are accepted by the recipient indefinitely.
3. Allografts/Homografts: Grafts from a donor to a recipient of the same species. Allografts are usually rejected unless special efforts are made to prevent this.
4. Xenografts/Heterografts: Grafts between different species. Such are usually destroyed very quickly by the recipient.

Skin Grafting. Most skin grafting at the present time is done with autografts. Again, they are not prone to rejection.

Corneal Transplants. Corneal transplants are allografts that may survive indefinitely without rejection. The cornea, however, must be removed from the donor within six hours after death and should be transplanted within twenty-four hours. The graft bed to which the cornea is transplanted usually has no blood supply. Furthermore, nourishment for the cornea comes directly by diffusion from the tissues. Since most rejection factors are carried in the blood stream, the lack of blood vessels to the cornea aids indefinite survival. In fact, it is reported that transplants are ninety percent successful in cases of the most common corneal diseases. Eyes can be donated by way of a "Uniform Donor's Card" (explained later), or an eye-donor pledge card from your local Eye-Bank. The Eye-Bank prefers that donors utilize the Eye-Donor pledge card

whenever possible. Unlike other transplant organizations, Eye-Banks
wish to maintain a file of those who have signed eye-donor pledge
cards. The only way that they can maintain such a file is if the donor
signs his card and returns the appropriate portion. The text for pledge
cards varies among eye-banks. Following is the pledge card and procedure for completion that is used by The Eye-Bank for Sight Restoration,
Inc., of New York.

Return this portion of the eye-pledge card to The Eye-Bank.
You may make a contribution with your eye-pledge by using the enclosed envelope.

Please Print

Last Name _____ First _____ M. ____

I am 18 years or more of age.   Street _____

I hereby make this anatomical gift to
take effect upon my death. I donate   City _____
my eyes to The Eye-Bank for Sight
Restoration, Inc., for any purpose
authorized by law.   State _____ Zip _____

Signed by the Donor in the presence
of the following who sign as witnesses.   Signature of Donor _____ Date ____

Witness _____ Date ____

Witness _____ Date ____

Keep this portion of the card with you always.

I AM AN EYE DONOR   Date ____

Please Print   Name ____ Address ____
Signature ____

My next-of-kin is:
Name ____ Relationship ____ Address ____

see other side

The procedure for use of the Eye-Bank card is important not only for
you, but for the organization that maintains files of all eye donors. The
following five steps should be helpful if you wish to donate.

1. Fill in both sections of the enclosed eye-donor pledge card. Sign the
   postcard-size part in the presence of two witnesses over eighteen years
   of age. They should then sign on the two lines marked *witness*. (If you
   are a minor, an eye-donor pledge card must be witnessed by your parents or legal guardians, stating their relationship).

2. Return the post-card size part to the Eye-Bank for its file, and keep the
   small part in your purse or wallet.

3. You should tell your family, lawyer, and doctor of your wish to have
   your eyes go to The Eye-Bank after death for sight-restoring transplants
   and/or for research on the prevention of blindness.

4. At the time of your death, all that is necessary is for the attending doctor,
   member of the family, or friend to call the Eye-Bank and give your name
   and the address of the hospital, funeral home, or private home where
   you are located.

5. The Eye-Bank removes the signed eye-donor card from the file and
   sends an ophthalmic surgeon or trained ophthalmic technician to the
   hospital, funeral home, or private home to remove the eyes. They are

returned by him to the Eye-Bank where they are examined and relayed as quickly as possible to the ophthalmic surgeon next on the waiting list. Speed is essential as twenty-four hours is the maximum desired time from the donor to the donee.

The Eye-Bank never charges for any of its services as it is supported by contributions and income from legacies. Likewise, the eyes of a donor are supplied free of charge to ophthalmic surgeons for sight-restoring transplants. You can donate your eyes to the Eye-Bank whatever your age and whether or not you wear glasses or have had an eye disease or surgery. It is estimated by the Eye-Bank for Sight Restoration that five times the current number of corneas donated are needed in the New York area alone.

Blood Vessel Transplants. The most successful blood vessel transplants are autografts. One of the most common reasons for these transplants is arteriosclerosis (hardening of the arteries). Vein transplants and arterial allografts are far less successful than are autografts.

Heart Valve Transplants. If a valve of the heart is seriously damaged, it can be replaced with an allograft though it is now possible to use manufactured valves.

Bone Transplants. If fractures fail to unite, autografts of bone can be extremely valuable in the healing process. It is estimated that thirty to forty thousand people require some form of bone transplantation each year.

Bone Marrow Transplants. The potential value of these transplants will not be realized until allograft rejection can more effectively be controlled. Perhaps then a wide variety of diseases of blood forming tissues may be treated by bone marrow transplantation.

Organ transplants are the result of relatively new surgical procedures. The first complete records of such transplants were not begun until 1953. While organ transplants are understandably more difficult to perform than are most other grafts, success has not been disappointing. Failures did exist in the beginning, but eventually many of the operations became standard practice and the success rate improved.

The Organ Transplant Registry in Chicago, Illinois keeps a tally on relevant transplantation data. By looking at the table below, you can identify the more successful organ transplants since 1953.

Table 1 TOTAL ORGAN TRANSPLANTS SINCE 1953

Organ	Total Operations	Recipients Still Alive as of 1976	Longest Survival in years
Heart	296	52	7.1
Liver	254	28	5.9
Lung	37	0	10 mths
Pancreas	47	1	3.5
Kidney	23,919	10,850	19

SOURCE: ACS/NIH Organ Transplant Registry. Chicago, Illinois, January 1, 1976.

This table may be broken down into the following, giving us an understanding of when the first heart, liver, lung, pancreas, and kidney transplants occurred. We can also identify increases or decreases in actual operations between the years of 1953 and 1976.

Table 2 WORLD TOTALS AND CHRONOLOGY OF ORGAN TRANSPLANTATION

Year	Heart	Liver	Lung	Pancreas	Kidney
1953–61					123
1962					67
1963		6	2		157
1964		4	0		359
1965		7	3		453
1966		3	1	2	561
1967	2	8	6	1	832
1968	101	39	6	6	1,245
1969	47	46	7	7	1,538
1970	17	31	2	9	1,990
1971	18	15	4	1	2,904
1972	18	23	3	5	3,486
1973	33	24	2	5	3,828
1974	29	30	0	7	3,620
1975	31	18	1	4	2,756
Total	296	254	37	47	23,919

SOURCE: ACS/NIH Organ Transplant Registry. Chicago, Illinois, January 1, 1976.

Kidney Transplants. The first attempt to transplant a kidney occurred in 1947. In fact, this was the first time an entire organ had ever been transplanted from one person to another. Since that time, the number of kidney transplants has increased steadily. At the present time, over two thousand kidneys are transplanted each year in the United States. Dr. Samuel L. Kountz of the State University Hospital in Brooklyn, New York estimates that less than one-tenth of the needed kidney donors are currently registered.

Success is far more prevalent today than ever before for three major reasons. First of all, rejection is minimized by improved methods of matching donor and recipient. In fact, a new test developed by Dr. Bach and his associates at the University of Wisconsin is said to further improve the possibility of matching. Called the P.L.T. test (primed lymphocyte test), it is a new tissue typing measure to ensure that the tissues of the donor are matched as perfectly as possible to those of the recipient for organs such as kidneys or tissue like bone marrow. The potential of this new test is being explored at the present time. Second, life is being sustained by artificial kidney machines until such time as matching is certain. Last, medical and technological advances have provided methods of preserving kidneys outside the human body, hence, more kidneys are available for transplanting. Kidneys can be kept viable for seventy hours but must be removed within thirty minutes of the cessation of heartbeat.

Kidney transplants are so commonplace today that some patients have received more than one transplant. In fact, it is noted that one patient has received as many as five. It is estimated that about thirty-five hundred kidney transplants will be performed in the United States during the current year. Physicians see a time, not too distant in the future, when ten to twenty thousand kidneys will be needed each year in the United States. The figure of thirty-five hundred is said to be less than one-half the number that are urgently needed. Those suffering from little or no kidney function must be kept alive with a dialysis (artificial kidney) machine. They may have to use this machine for two to three years until a suitably matched donor kidney is available. The annual cost for dialysis use approaches twenty thousand dollars. Less expensive "home" machines are available, but they are also less efficient. The problem now is that there are more people with kidney malfunction than there are kidney machines. The result is obvious; many die before they ever get to use a kidney machine. The solution is also obvious; greater kidney donation by those approaching death is needed.

Liver Transplants. Liver transplants rank third in effectiveness among major organ transplants. The liver itself is a complicated organ that serves nearly three dozen functions concerned with the processes of nutrition, digestion, and red blood cell development. It is, in effect, a chemical factory; this has much to do with its failure rate.

Heart Transplants. Many of us remember that the first successful heart transplant was performed in 1967 by Dr. Christian Barnard in South Africa. Other surgeons from twenty-one different countries attempted the same operation during and after 1967. The peak year for heart transplants (the year during which the most were performed) was 1968, the year following Dr. Bernard's triumphant breakthrough. Most of the patients died soon after the time the surgery was performed; subsequently, medical enthusiasm dropped. Recently techniques and procedures of the operation have been improved. There are indications that such transplants, as a last resort to bypassing clotted arteries, replacing damaged valves, and installing pacemakers, are once again receiving medical attention and increased enthusiasm. By examining the following table, we can identify the countries and years heart transplant operations were performed and how their success is becoming more evident.

Table 3   CHRONOLOGY AND WORLD DISTRIBUTION OF HUMAN HEART TRANSPLANTATION

Year	World Totals	U.S.A.	Canada	France	South Africa	Other Countries[a]
1967	2	1	0	0	1	0
1968	101(2)	54(1)[b]	14	10(1)	2	21
1969	47(2)	34(1)	1	0	4(1)	8
1970	17(3)	16(3)	1	0	0	0
1971	18(3)	13(2)	1	0	3(1)	1
1972	18(5)	15(5)	0	0	2	1
1973	33(6)	21(5)	1	8(1)	2	2
1974	29(12)	17(9)	0	9(3)	1	2
1975	31(19)	23(16)	0	5(2)	2(1)	1
Total	296(52)	194(42)	18	32(7)	16(3)	36

[a]Argentina, Australia, Belgium, Brazil, Chile, Czechoslovakia, England, Germany, India, Israel, Japan, Peru, Poland, Spain, Switzerland, Turkey, U.S.S.R., Venezuela.
[b]Numbers in parenthesis indicate number of recipients living on January 1, 1976.
SOURCE: ACS/NIH Organ Transplant Registry. Chicago, Illinois, January 1, 1976.

The percentage of success for transplanting organs such as the lungs or pancreas is low in comparison to that of the kidney, heart, and liver. However, as medical knowledge and techniques advance, such operations will one day become standard procedure. Still, a number of problems will exist even after the problem of rejection is mastered. These problems can best be summarized as supply v. demand and ethical and moral considerations.

Assuming that medical science will one day advance to a point where all transplantations are common practice (and we have no reason to doubt such eventual advancement), where will all the needed organs come from? If we are short of donors now, what will the future hold? Demand now exceeds supply. What will happen in the future? This aspect of transplantation introduces moral and ethical considerations. Will there be a black market for transplants? What effect will money or political power play in the process? What about the existing controversy over the point at which death occurs? Death must take place legally before certain organs are removed. Would a physician consent to diagnose death "early" so that organs could be removed for increased probability of success in transplantation? All of these factors will definitely be concerns of the future.

The Brain Transplant? Science fiction writers have long predicted technological advances, perhaps unknowingly, but somewhat accurately. Trips to the moon, heart transplants, and now, brain transplants? Impossible you say! Not long ago, heart transplants seemed as remote as did trips to the moon. A pill to prevent pregnancy? Impossible! But all now exist. Perhaps people whose minds are still functioning effectively will someday have an alternative to physical death. Perhaps sustaining life through a brain transplant to a body whose brain is irrepairably damaged will be possible. Or perhaps life will be sustained by transplanting a brain into a mechanical apparatus. Perhaps, perhaps, perhaps. While nothing is really impossible, it may be improbable in varying degrees.

How improbable are brain transplants? Dr. Robert J. White, chief neurosurgeon at Cleveland Metropolitan General Hospital, has done ten successful head transplants on monkeys. While the most successful lived only thirty-six hours, the head-transplanted monkeys retained their ability to see, smell, taste, hear, move their faces, close their eyes, and feel pain in the facial region. Although Dr. White's purposes were different than those suggested here, the result is a significant statement supportive of the future of brain transplants. The issue, however, is not really one of medical-scientific-technological advancement. Instead, it appears to be a question of ethics.

Donation—How Do I Donate My Body Or Part Of It? It has been suggested that many years ago bodies for medical research were so scarce that doctors would pay people to rob graves. This is not difficult to understand (morbid, perhaps, but not difficult) if one considers man's insatiable thirst for knowledge. Because of the strict religious beliefs and codes of the past, it was unheard of to donate any part of the human body after death to be cut up and studied at the end of a doctor's scalpel. The search for knowledge was not considered.

Obviously, at the present time some people feel that the greatest gift they have to offer to humanity is their body. Even in death they serve others with their gift. In effect, the human body after death can serve for purposes of transplantation or medical education. Either way, it may be seen as a gift to future society. Evidence suggests that many people feel this way. The number of body donations has increased from 69 in 1966–67, to 221 in 1973–74. Some areas of the United States report long lists of body donations. Others report the opposite. A Gallup Poll conducted in January of 1968 indicated that seventy percent of all Americans would willingly donate their organs to medical science after death. However, the percentage actually doing so is far less.

In the past medical schools received specimens from unclaimed bodies. This number has decreased from 354 in 1966–67 to only 140 in 1973–74. This decrease may be due to Social Security benefits. Bodies that would have been left to the state for disposal because of financial problems are now taken care of by a death payment that more and more people are eligible for.

The largest problem regarding body donation is a legal technicality. Legally, there must be a written statement from the person showing his intentions. Before 1968 each state had different laws governing the donation of a body. Then, in 1968, the Uniform Anatomical Gift Act was introduced and later passed in each state. This act eliminated all legal and ethnic barriers. In simple terms, it stated that anyone eighteen years or older could donate all or parts of his body for research, transplantation, or placement in a tissue bank. It also required each person wishing donation to carry a card on his person stating what is to be donated. This card must be signed in the presence of two people (witnesses). Additionally, in the case of transplantation, the time of death must be determined by a physician who is not a member of the transplant team. If the donor has not acted in his lifetime, his survivors or next of kin may act for him, i.e., they may donate his body. However, if a donor has acted and has signed a valid donor's card, his desire is paramount to the rights of all others. Only state autopsy law takes precedence over the donor's rights. Finally, the donor can, anytime prior to death, revoke the gift, or the gift can be rejected. The need for your body depends on circumstances such as time, place, and circumstances of death. Usually, a body will not be accepted for the purpose of medical education if any organ or tissue, other than corneas for the eye-bank, has been removed. The Uniform Donor Card can be obtained from any medical society (AMA, Humanity Gifts Registry, etc.). A sample of this card is shown at the top of the next page.

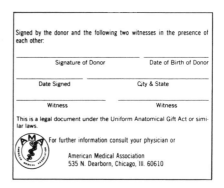

In addition to holding a donor's card, your desire to donate your body to science should be mentioned in your will. While it is not required to mention this gift in your will if you have signed a valid donor's card, it is recommended. It is also recommended that you make your intentions clear to your physician and to as many relatives and friends as possible.

Money is not, nor can it be, exchanged for making an anatomical donation. Upon death, your body will be transferred to a medical facility. You may arrange for it to be donated to a specific institution. If you wish it to go to a medical school, it will be used to provide instruction for future doctors. These cadavers are used for the betterment of the medical profession, and indirectly, the betterment of society. If you wish your body to go to a mortician school, it will be used in the training program for morticians. If you decide to donate organs, your body is taken to a hospital where the organs you have donated are removed and temporarily stored or used in transplants.

An estimated two hundred thousand Americans have made arrangements to donate their bodies, or parts of them, to science. Perhaps this is because of increasing funeral costs, or perhaps because of growing humanitarianism. Whatever the reason, the resulting benefits are incalculable.

Because the time factor is so crucial in many transplants, and since many lives are lost in auto accidents, many states are now considering putting a donor format on the back of the driver's license. (California has already done so.) This would give all drivers an opportunity to donate their bodies or parts of them in the case of death by accident. An alternative to this that has been suggested is a take-off on a current British idea. They label the idea "contracting out." They simply suggest that those people who *do not* want their organs transplanted after death should sign and carry a card. All others would be presumed to have given consent. In the United States, we could put such a statement on the back of a driver's license. It could simply read "I do not wish to donate any part of my body after death." With a place for a signature, the form would be complete. If you had signed it, organs would not be used after your death. If you had not signed it, any and/or all body parts could be used. This procedure of "contracting out" would most likely result in an increase in the number of available organs and tissues for at least one reason. Since our society is death denying and we cannot actually believe we are going to die, the result would be that we would neglect to sign the card, leaving it for a later date. Once your entire body had been used, the institution would dispose of it by cremation. If just an organ or so was involved, the body could be returned. (The family would pay for funeral arrangements.) However, the thought is not so much one of expense as it is of humanitary contribution.

As we look at various religious attitudes regarding donations in a later chapter, let us summarize the situation. Only Jehovah's Witnesses and Orthodox Jews forbid or restrict donation of the body or its parts. Many other religions actually encourage their members to donate. If you are in doubt as to how your religion treats the subject, it is best to contact your pastor, priest, or rabbi.

SUMMARY

Fear of premature burial was *a realistic fear in the earlier days in the United States, and it still is a real fear in some other parts of the world. This fear led to extreme experiments and procedures to prove death or provide for escape from the casket once buried alive. Embalming, which appears to have removed this fear in the United States, is not generally practiced in other countries.*

Defining death is not a simple task. Part of the problem is that death is not a point in time; it is a process. There are three main phases to this process including Clinical Death, Brain Death, and Cellular Death.

The most widely accepted description of death at the present time is that proposed by the Harvard University Committee. Defining death becomes an important concern when transplantation enters the picture. Although it is not a new procedure (it was practiced around 600 B.C.), transplanting today is becoming more successful as researchers are beginning to control the rejection factor.

Because of recent legislation, anyone over eighteen years of age can legally donate their body, or any part of it, for transplantation and/or research. Many of us "say" we will donate our bodies or parts of them but fail to sign a legal donor's card. Perhaps this is based on our inability to accept our in-

evitable deaths. Hence, we put the signing of the card off. Legally, medically, and religiously, there are few roadblocks standing in the way of donation.

NOTES
---

1. "Buried Alive," *British Medical Journal,* 2 (December 8, 1887), 819.
2. "Real and Apparent Death," *Lancet,* 1 (January 29, 1887), 233.
3. W. Tebb and E. P. Vollum, *Premature Burial* (London: Swan Lonnenschen and Co., Ltd., 1905), pp. 81–82.
4. "The Growing Practice of Premature Burial," *Current Literature,* 43 (December 1907), 682.
5. Tebb and Vollum, *Premature Burial,* p. 346.
6. Le Darnici-France, Graf. V. Karnicki, Betracheungen ub Lethargie ad. Scheintod U. Kurtz Beschribg. d. patentirten Rettungsmittel 'Karnice', trans. John D. Arnold, Thomas F. Zimmerman, and Daniel C. Martin, in "Public Attitudes and the Diagnosis of Death," *Journal of the American Medical Association,* 206, no. 9 (November 25, 1968), 1952–53.
7. *Oshkosh Daily Northwestern* (Oshkosh, Wisconsin), December 10, 1975, p. 9, col. 1.
8. American Medical Association, *Proceedings of the AMA House of Delegates,* December 2–5, 1973, p. 345, June 23–27, 1974, p. 345, December 1–4, 1974, p. 303. Reprinted by permission of the American Medical Association.

SELECTED BIBLIOGRAPHY

AMERICAN MEDICAL ASSOCIATION, *Donation of Bodies or Organs for Transplantation and Medical Science.* (Pamphlet OP-371).

"Boy Died After Nine Year Coma," *Oshkosh Daily Northwestern,* (Oshkosh, Wisconsin), December 10, 1975, p. 9, col. 1.

"Buried Alive," *British Medical Journal,* 2 (December 8, 1887), 819.

"Definition of Irreversible Coma," *American Medical Association Journal,* 205, no. 6 (August 5, 1968), pp. 337–40.

FREESE, ARTHUR S., "What's the Future for Human Transplants?" *Science Digest,* 71, no. 6 (June 1972), 9–14.

"The Growing Practice of Premature Burial," *Current Literature,* 43 (December 1907), 680–682.

HENDIN, DAVID, *Death As a Fact of Life,* pp. 43–57. New York: Warner Paperback Library, 1974.

MAGUIRE, DANIEL C., *Death by Choice,* p. 17. Garden City, N.Y.: Doubleday and Company, Inc., 1974.

MORISON, ROBERT S., "Dying," in *Life and Death in Medicine* (San Francisco: W.H. Freeman and Co., 1973), p. vi.

PRIAL, FRANK J., "In Transplant of Kidneys," *New York Times,* March 8, 1975, p. 29, col. 7.

"The Problem of Burial Alive," *Current Literature,* 39 (July 1905), 66–67.

"Real and Apparent Death," *Lancet,* 1 (January 29, 1887), 233.

SCHMECK, HAROLD M., "Kidney Transplant Survival is Linked to Tissue," *New York Times,* August 19, 1975, p. 30, col. 5.

SMIRNOW, VIRGIL, "The Real Truth About Kidney Transplants," Pamphlet. (Washington, D.C.: September 1973), p. 1.

TAYLOR, CHARLOTTE, "Donating Your Body to Science," Pamphlet. (New York: The Foundation For The Advancement Of Medical Knowledge).

TEBB, W., and E. P. VOLLUM, *Premature Burial* pp. 81–82, 346. London: Swan Lonnenschen and Co., Ltd., 1905.

"The Transposed Head," *Newsweek,* 82, no. 23 (December 3, 1973), 79–80.

"Transplants," *The New Encyclopedia Britannica* (1974), 18, 627–32.

"Whatever Happened To... Drive to Transplant Vital Human Organs?" *U.S. News and World Reports,* (September 10, 1973), 46.

4

The Future of Aging and Degenerative and Terminal Disorders

Age is a quality of mind.
If you have left your dreams behind,
If hope is cold,
If you no longer look ahead,
If your ambitions' fires are dead
Then you are old.
But if from life you take the best,
If in life you keep the jest,
If love you hold;
No matter how the years go by,
No matter how the birthdays fly
You are not old.

(H.S. FRITSCH "How Old Are You?")

The Problem of Growing Old—(or must we?). Gerontology is the scientific study of aging and those problems associated with it. We may conceive of aging in terms of movement toward that final inevitable end. Science has done much to extend the life expectancy of the masses over the last half-century. Is it possible to eliminate old age or to "cure" death? Dr. Lyall Watson claims that clinical death is purely a theoretical construct. Now that medical technology is approaching that point where all vital functions may be able to be maintained or replaced, death may be postponed almost indefinitely. By looking at death as a disease, we can understand that it may, in fact, be temporary and responsive to cure. Supporting Watson's belief, Edgar N. Jackson reported on a sociological survey in California that indicated that the majority of persons felt death was a form of illness that could be overcome through medical research. Perhaps it is! Dr. Leonard Hayflick and his fellow researchers at Stanford University have conducted experiments that seem to indicate that the nucleus of each cell holds the secrets of aging. Apparently, the nucleus acts as a "clock," determining how many times a cell will divide. The theory goes that as one ages, cells divide at a lesser rate.

In yet another approach to the "disease" of aging, Dr. William H. Adler of the National Institute on Aging in Baltimore, looks to hormones to counter the effects of aging. Adler states that there is evidence that suggests that a thymus-related part, which generates "warriors" to fight invaders for protection through immunity, weakens as one gets older and produces a lesser quantity of one of its hormones. As this theory is developed, administration of this hormone could alter the rate of aging.

For the time being, however, all of us will age. As our age increases,

54

so does the probability of our developing degenerative and terminal disorders and/or diseases. How would we feel? What would or should we do in such cases?

Degenerative or Terminal Disorders. Telling a patient that he is going to die is usually done by his physician, if it is done at all. In some cases the physician may tell the family; they are, in turn, expected to tell the patient. This knowledge places the patient in control of his life. Unfortunately, most physicians are not trained to deal with death psychologically. As a result, many terminally ill patients are not told of their inevitable deaths. Feifel estimates that between sixty-nine and ninety percent of all physicians prefer not to tell their patients that they are dying. Many authorities suggest, however, that withholding this information forces the patient to die alone and in isolation. This is unfortunate because even children pick up verbal and nonverbal cues. Glasser and Strauss suggest that there are four types of 'awareness contexts' surrounding the terminal patient, members of the hospital staff, and members of the patient's family. The first is termed 'closed awareness' and refers to a situation in which the patient is totally unaware of his fatal illness. The second awareness context is called 'suspicion awareness' and is described as a situation in which the patient suspects he is dying and attempts to confirm his suspicion although those around him try not to let him find out. The third type of awareness context is known as 'mutual pretense awareness'. In this situation, everyone knows of the impending death, including the patient, but all try to avoid discussion of the subject as though it were not going to happen. The fourth and final type of awareness context is 'open awareness'. In this situation everyone knows about the impending death and talking about it is frequent.

In 'closed awareness' there is a definite strain put on the relationships between the patient, his family, and hospital staff members because everyone involved attempts to guard the secret. In 'suspicion awareness' a contest takes place between the patient and those involved as he attempts to find the truth. In 'mutual pretense awareness' fear of death forces those involved to restrain conversation as though death could be avoided. In 'open awareness' the truth is on the table. Many authorities believe this to be the best situation because it affords the dying patient the greatest amount of dignity. The question of when to tell the patient is of utmost importance. The physician must be able to communicate the truth, often in stages, at the appropriate times. Additionally, some hope can be maintained by referring to recent medical developments. It is important, however, that this approach not become routine as it is always different depending on the individual's illness.

In reality, most terminally ill patients, including children, know they are going to die before they are even told. People react differently toward them or situations appear different. A number of these changes result in a victim's knowing of his death. Upon being told of his death, the victim can discuss it and perhaps make his last days meaningful. Children, as well as adults have the right to die in dignity. It is this "death with dignity" factor that has resulted in concern over the emotional state of a dying patient. Obviously, some people are concerned. William Roberts and James Rosner have founded a new service for helping dying patients. Called Threshold Research Center on Death and Dying, Inc., the Westwood, California firm provides specially trained companions for seriously ill or dying persons. The firm supplies someone who listens to the dying patient with a sympathetic ear for $7.50 an hour. The organizers affirm that Threshold is a profit-making organization that, like others in our free enterprise system, supplies a service and answers a need.

A similar service opened in Berkeley, California on February 1, 1975. Unlike Threshold, it is a phone service operated by volunteers. Offering information and companionship, all a dying person need do is call. It was organized by Charles Garfield, a psychologist who teaches a thanatology course at the University of California. Dr. Garfield has arranged for professionals who deal with the dying to serve as volunteers. Additionally, each of the volunteers attends classes and training sessions that explore personal attitudes toward death. This is believed to be the first nonprofit service for the dying.

Dealing with the inevitable death of a terminally ill patient is always difficult. We tend to perceive such a person as neither alive nor dead. While he may be physiologically alive, he is nonetheless suffering social death. This tragedy becomes even more traumatic when the terminally ill individual is a child. We perceive an analogy between life and children. Therefore, when we consider that a child may soon die from a terminal illness, we tend to help him deny the inevitable.

We help a dying child deny his inevitable end mainly because we feel guilty and helpless toward the situation. Reasons for parental difficulty range from inability to understand the death concept to the reminder that death is a threat to their own mortalities. As a result, parents become 'overly-nice' to the child. They try to do things for him that they normally would not do. But children are smarter than parents, or even doctors, suppose them to be. They recognize certain changes in people's behavior and know when something is wrong. Unfortunately, the child reacts by carrying the burden of his illness alone. He does not wish to hurt his family or make the hospital staff uncomfortable. In the final analysis, however, it is the parents who often have the greater difficulty in dealing with the impending death of a child.

Furthermore, hospitalized children are exposed to at least three environmental stresses: separation from their mothers, some relatively new and traumatic medical procedures, and the occurrence of death around them. The anxiety associated with each stage is dependent upon the child's age. From infancy to about five years of age, separation from the mother results in the greatest anxiety. For children five to ten years of age, traumatic procedures are the most upsetting. And for children over ten, it is the death of others that creates the greatest amount of anxiety.

The most common fears of children who are terminally ill are not knowing when they will die, fearing pain, fearing the unknown, missing their family and friends, and being missed by their family and friends. If the channels of communication are opened, much of the fear and anxiety can be relieved.

It is usually best for the terminally ill patient, child or adult, to be told of his condition. There are exceptions to this belief and each case must be treated individually. A general statement supporting telling all dying patients of their disease is difficult if not impossible. If told that a loved one is dying, it is best for both family and friends to accept his death and work with him. Finally, it is best for the dying patient to stay actively involved in matters that he was involved in before he knew of his condition. Time should be used creatively because a person can and should feel a sense of worth in his last days of life.

Helping those who are aging or terminally ill has been a concern of many groups as well as individuals. In 1972 the United States Senate held a Special Committee on Aging. One of the topics that received attention was the concept of a *hospice*. A dictionary defines *hospice* as "a lodging for travelers or for young persons or the underprivileged."[1] The meaning has been altered slightly so that now *hospice* implies a health delivery system that helps patients round out their lives and live with meaning even though they are dying of a degenerative, irreversible disease. Reverend Edward F. Dobihal, Jr., chairman of the Hospice Planning Group (a group that has received a state charter to plan a hospice in the United States), explained that the system will include care at home as well as in an inpatient setting. This is not really a new concept as hospices existed in France, Germany, and other places in the 1500s. However, they were forgotten until St. Joseph's was organized in 1902 by a religious foundation in London, England. With St. Joseph's still operating and the need for facilities increasing, a new hospice has just opened in Sheffield, England. Meanwhile, in the United States, a hospice has been organized in New Haven, Connecticut. It provides coordinated home and hospital health care to dying patients and their families. In the near future, they plan to open up a medical facility of their own based on the philosophy with which they now operate. Meanwhile, approximately forty-three others are in some stage of planning.

The most frequently asked question is "What can a hospice do that a conventional hospital cannot?" To answer this question, it is easiest to explain the conventional care terminal patients receive in a hospital, and to compare it to the type of care they need (and that can be provided by a hospice).

First of all, terminal patients in a hospital are usually shuttled back and forth between doctors, wings, even hospitals. What most of these patients need is consistency. They also need someone to help them maintain the balance that they want in their lives. It is balance that they feel they are losing in a conventional hospital.

Second, hospitals are structured toward cure, even in cases of terminal illness. This goal is unrealistic for many. Those that are going to die, know they are going to die, and accept their inevitable fates need another type of help. Hospitals generally do very little to help people in this situation. Adding to this concern is the manner in which hospitals strive for cure. Reverand Dobihal, among others, is concerned about the heavy use of drugs in terminal cases. It is not uncommon to see many patients knocked out by medication. Surely this is an inappropriate way to prevent pain since it robs the patient of the little time he has left. The goal is for the patient to receive only the necessary amount of pain relief so he can still be alert and do those things he feels he wants to or would do in the time that he has left.

Third, hospitals typically refer and relate only to the patient and his cure. The concept of hospices is built around the patient and his family. Hospitals make it difficult for the family to stay together through visiting procedures (Who can visit? How long? How often?) The hospice wants to help the family stay together, or at least go through the experience together. Reverand Dobihal relates an example of a woman who was visiting her husband in an English hospice. "She was able to bring him special food that she had prepared at home. The grandchildren came to visit. They could even bring pets in. This kind of maintenance and support is quite possible but it is not possible in present systems."[2] Senator Frank Church, of Idaho, adds, "I know the last hospital I was in refused to have any dealings with children under sixteen years of age."[3] The hospice hopes to include family members in the entire process whether the patient is at home or in the inpatient facility. Hospice, Inc.

outlines the types of family involvement deemed necessary in the final stages of a person's terminal illness:

1. Training family members to participate in the treatment
2. Encouraging them to do such things as cooking special meals for the patient (very important for ethnic groups and to stimulate appetite)
3. Having unlimited visiting so that the total family unit, including children, can participate
4. Providing special space for families to meet each other and space in which family members may live when death is imminent
5. Providing special social and educational programs for the family and patient, with these continuing for the family after death has occurred

In summary, the hospice is set up as a multidimensional concept offering care for terminally ill patients both at home and in their own inpatient unit. Heroic measures to sustain life at any cost are not used. Antibiotics, radiation therapy, resuscitators, and cardiac massage are foreign to the hospice environment. The only medications given to hospice patients are painkillers. The various personnel of the hospice aid the maintenance of life *with* the disease; they don't cure it. Hospice physicians and nurses are trained to provide appropriate care, make home visits, see family and patients, care for inpatients, and work *with* family physicians. The hospice, a terminal care facility, helps the patient to be a person who may live out his life in the manner of his choosing.

A hospital or institution where terminally ill patients reside obviously affects the quality of life of their patients. A good example, however atypical, is Memorial-Sloan Kettering, which is the largest private cancer center in the world. The purpose of the center is to combat cancer of all types through the care and study of patients. A climate of creative interaction is maintained between those engaged in scientific investigation and patient care. The new 563-bed hospital in New York City combines the most advanced technology with the latest concepts in humanitarian service to over thirteen thousand inpatients and one hundred thousand outpatients a year. The hospital accepts patients from every country, and medical personnel from all over the world train at the hospital. Once trained, they work all over the world.

The physical setting of the pediatric ward is very comfortable, pleasant, and flexible. The rooms are brightly painted and personal objects are allowed. It is believed that this offers a more secure atmosphere for the child. Rooms are shared between two persons, usually of the same age group, unless physical condition warrants a private room. One room described by an observer was shared by two teenagers. One wall was covered with posters, stuffed animals were smiling, and the girls were helping each other paint their nails. Each room had individual television sets, radios, telephones, and bathing facilities.

The playroom was very spacious and bicycles and toys were in use. There was an adjustable pool table for those confined to wheel chairs. The full time recreational therapist was speaking with a very depressed little girl who sat in a wheel chair with one hand supporting her balding head and the other supporting i.v. apparatus. There was a garden where the children participate in biological projects.

The philosophy of the staff is one of hope because within the last few years new hope has been found for cancer patients. Since the family seeks treatment to keep the child active and alive, it is the nursing staff that deals realistically and honestly with the patient and his family. It is felt that the patient has the right to live as comfortably as possible. Working as a team, the staff's philosophy stresses total family care, and the nurse works to meet the psychosocial, learning, and rehabilitation needs of the child and his family. Hope is transferred by the nurses' attitudes as the child is treated, and through the rapport that is developed with family members.

Rap sessions enable the children to air their feelings. Adolescents meet once a month with the social worker and head or staff nurse. The only prerequisite for attending the sessions is that the child know his diagnosis. Here the child talks about his feelings, concerns, peer relationships, and anything else that may develop. One of the ways that a nurse can find out how the child views his disease is to ask him why he is at the hospital. In this way the nurse can assess if he is accepting what he already knows. Another means is through hospital play, primarily used with younger children. Here the child can reenact some of his fears. The nurse can use this time to clarify his feelings and fantasies and to assess where the patient is in relation to his feelings.

Judging by the progress of most of the children, reflective play seems to be the most effective. This is a procedure where the nurse becomes the patient and the child becomes the nurse. The child is allowed to use play needles to stick the nurse and observe her reactions. Through this play the child is able to vent his anger and see that it is acceptable to be afraid and cry, as the nurse might do this when she receives the "needle". This also enables the nurse to pick up other clues about his fears. After each session, the social worker and nurse evaluate the progress of the children and keep flow sheets or summary behavior inventories. These are then available for other staff members to use in planning necessary care for each patient.

Children suffering from a terminal illness do not usually ask if they are going to die. They usually tend to talk in symbols, so a nurse must be a good listener and be alert for signs of fear and anxiety. The nurse might find that the child does not sleep at night or that he suddenly wants a night light. This usually indicates a fear of separation or abandonment.

The parents meet once a week with the social worker. Here they are able to gain support from other parents who are experiencing the same anxieties and fears. Other terminal centers, as well as general hospitals, would do well to copy the model set up by Memorial-Sloan Kettering.

Stages. Technological advancement has created an illusion. Simply stated, medicine can postpone the death of people indefinitely. This is not a very realistic way of perceiving the world. Surely some of us will die "before our time," and we may want to know more about this possibility. It has been suggested that in our unconscious minds, we can only be killed, i.e., it is inconceivable to die of a natural cause. Hence, most of us feel as though we will never die. How do we react when we find out we are going to die? How do we react when we find out someone close to us is going to die?

Dr. Elisabeth Kubler-Ross, a leader in psychiatric theory regarding dying patients, suggests that each dying individual, if he or she receives appropriate psychiatric care, will pass through five stages. Although the stages hold no magical knowledge in themselves, it is important to realize that there are things that we, as close friends, can do to help. Imagine your closest friend (we'll call her Ronnie) has just found out that she is dying of terminal cancer. What can you expect? What can you do? Keep in mind that we are offering a rather simplified version of the five stages a terminally ill patient may pass through. These "stages" may occur in order, out of order, even reoccur. Furthermore, the description of each stage is minimal, i.e., other reactions occur depending on the individual who is passing through these stages.

The first stage is termed Shock and Denial. It is also sometimes called the "no, not me" stage. Ronnie may wander from physician to physician looking for one who will tell her that nothing is wrong, searching for responses that say she'll be OK with time or that she will live. As a friend, the most important thing you can do is analyze the problem. Is it really Ronnie denying death, or you? You should make yourself available at any time Ronnie wants you. She will want to talk about it and you should be there to listen.

After a short time, Ronnie will pass into the second stage, the "why me" or Anger and Rage stage. Its very name describes its characteristics. In this stage Ronnie may yell at anyone who is around at the time. It may be you, the doctor, the nurse, anyone. Do not set yourself up as a judge in this situation. The very fact that Ronnie has decided to yell at you should be taken as a compliment. Do not forget, she has every reason to feel this way. She is losing exactly what you have, life. Let her vent her feelings.

Now, Ronnie passes into the third stage, called the Bargaining stage. Outwardly, Ronnie looks happy, content, peaceful. Inwardly, however, Ronnie is still afraid, still upset over her eventual loss. She wants an extension, just a little more time to do the things she must or always wanted to do. She will bargain with doctors, nurses, you, even God. "A little more time," she says, "and then I will go peaceably." Help Ronnie make her arrangements. Help her make out her will. The very fact that she wants you to help her is an indication that she is making progress towards acceptance.

Suddenly, almost overnight, things seem different. Ronnie starts talking about the things she has failed to do in life. This is the first sign of Depression, the fourth stage. Later, Ronnie becomes almost silent. She is mourning those things she will be unable to do. She may not want to see you because you remind her of her future losses. Outside interests dwindle as Ronnie finally chooses the one or two people with whom she wants to be until the end. You should look at it as a compliment if she chooses you. She will let you know in her own special way. Much of this fourth stage is difficult for Ronnie. It is even more difficult for men since, by tradition, they are not permitted to cry or show weakness. This is unfortunate since many men suffer more because of this. During this stage, you can help Ronnie feel that she is exhibiting normal, even courageous behavior. Allow her to cry it all out. Remember, you are only losing one person; she is losing many. If you help her through this stage, she will be better prepared to enter the final stage.

The final stage that Ronnie enters is not necessarily a happy one, but it is one that offers a feeling of inner and outer peace. It is termed Acceptance because it identifies a final "acceptance" of the inevitability of death. It is good for Ronnie to reach this stage before she dies. Ronnie can go another way. She can become resigned to her death and exhibit a feeling of bitterness or a "what's the use" attitude. Instead of just giving up and resigning, she can accept her death. She can be at peace with herself.

During this process of dying, we should be most concerned with the patient's mental or emotional status. It is this concern that brings up the initial question "Should we tell the dying patient that he is dying?" While there are many times when it is not possible to tell the patient, a minority of physicians believe that the patient has a basic right to know. Summarizing one physician's concern, "Being blunt is being cruel, but I certainly wouldn't beat around the bush with any answer to my patient's case. I try to be as straightforward as possible". But this physician is not in the majority. In fact a recent study pointed out that women want to know more than physicians want to tell them. When asked if a sixteen-year-old boy should be told he is dying, thirty-four percent of one thousand female subjects surveyed indicated "yes." With respect to the same question, only twelve percent of one hundred twenty physicians replied "yes." This result indicates a gap in doctor–patient relationships that must be resolved.

Those physicians who do believe in telling the patient of his inevitable demise do so in a way that gives the patient a basis for hope. Hope should always be present because a terminal disease or disorder may stop short of death. Remission in cancer victims is not completely unheard of.

Kubler-Ross indicates that you do not really help a person die, you help him live until he dies. However, until you yourself can face the topic of death, it is very difficult to help others. A patient can quickly sense your concept of death. If you walk into his room and talk about how pretty the flowers are, he will know that you do not want to talk about his impending death. As a result, he will not confide in you. His desire to do so must be of his own selection. It is important to his dignity that he chooses you, not that you appoint yourself. You should not feel rejected if the patient does not wish to confide in you. He does not usually want pity. What he does want is someone he can trust to *listen* to him.

A discussion of SIDS, (Sudden Infant Death Syndrome), has purposely been left for the close of this chapter. SIDS is a very special case of death that occurs in infants. It requires a special type of understanding and acceptance. Also called Crib Death and Sudden Unexplained Death (SUD), the syndrome causes the death of a child that is unexpected considering the medical history of that child. Additionally, the cause remains unexplained in over ninety percent of the deaths. It is truly a medical mystery that there is no way to predict or prevent it. An example of SIDS is the following: A four-month-old baby boy was in a car bed on the way to his grandmother's house. His mother turned around at a stoplight, five minutes into the ten minute trip, to pat her boy. Upon arriving at the house, the mother turned around to get her boy. He was dead.

This is an example of an experience that is not uncommon. There need be no warning signs or previous serious illness. Furthermore, there is no way of preventing it. Each year in the United States, about fifteen thousand mothers will put their apparently healthy babies to bed only to find them dead when they next check them. SIDS victims die quickly and quietly.

SIDS strikes about three out of every one thousand infants born in the United States. It is the leading cause of death among infants from one week to five months of age. The syndrome occurs most often in males between the second and fourth months of life, but it rarely occurs after the sixth month. Furthermore, it tends to occur most often in late autumn. Hence, conception of SIDS victims takes place predominantly in the winter, one year before death. It is not known if this factor plays a significant role in causing SIDS. Approximately sixty-five to eighty-five percent of all these deaths occur during the six coldest months of the year.

Incidence rates are highest among nonwhite babies, babies from low socioeconomic status families, babies living in crowded conditions, premature babies, and babies who have recently had colds. According to Geertinger, sudden unexplained death sometimes occurs in children who breast feed; however, the majority are artificially fed. While the cause of SIDS is still unknown, the rate of incidence has not been affected by advances in the fields of pediatrics or public health. Past research has established only two things. First, SIDS is a real disease entity; and second, SIDS is a disease that *can* be defined through autopsy. Through an autopsy, a pattern of hemorrhagic spots about the size of a pinhead show up in the lungs. Other signs found that indicate crib death are edema (fluid in the lungs), inflammation of the airway leading to the lungs, the heart is dilated, and the bladder is empty.

The tragedy of SIDS is compounded by an even greater tragedy, ignorance and misunderstanding. Parents, friends, relatives, and physicians are all guilty of compounding the distress. Because of lack of knowledge, public officials have actually held parents for murder after their babies died in a crib. Babysitters have been accused of carelessness when babies have died in their care. Worse yet, brothers and sisters have been tortured with guilt and prolonged suffering after having been told to watch their baby brother or sister. All of this occurs because of misinformation, or worse yet, lack of any information at all.

Parental, professional, and semiprofessional groups have been organized in many cities to aid each other as well as to inform the public (including members of the clergy, policemen, and firemen) about SIDS. Among these groups are the Washington Association for SIDS, based in Seattle, Washington, and the Guild for Infant Survival in Philadelphia, Pennsylvania and Baltimore, Maryland. The Seattle organization is active with volunteers who assist families through the traumatic experience of SIDS. Basically, it lets them know that they are not alone, that the baby did not suffer, and that they are not to blame.

If parents can understand the few facts we have concerning SIDS, perhaps their guilt feelings can be alleviated and acceptance of this type of death can be approached with a minimum of difficulty.

Gerontology is the study of aging. Some gerontologists perceive death as a disease that may be responsive to a cure the way other diseases are. Aging is a process that, for the greatest part of our population, is understood as that which preceeds dying and death.

Telling or not telling a terminally ill patient of his condition is a recent concern. Most physicians reportedly do not prefer to tell their terminal patients. Regardless, most terminal patients know of their inevitable deaths even before, or if, they are told. For some reason, physicians as well as relatives, wish to protect the terminally ill patient from this knowledge, especially if the patient is a child.

Hospices are being organized throughout the United States as an alternative to the more traditional hospital where terminally ill patients can reside until their deaths. Here, they can live until they die without the fear of being "kept alive" by extraordinary means.

Terminally ill patients may pass through five stages if they receive appropriate psychological care. These stages may occur in order, out of order, or even reoccur.

SIDS, Sudden Infant Death Syndrome, is a type of death that requires special understanding as its causes are still unknown.

NOTES

1. *Merriam Webster Dictionary,* 17th ed. (New York: Pocket Books, Simon and Schuster Division of Gulf and Western Corp., 1974), p. 341.
2. U.S., Congress, Senate, *Hearings Before The Special Committee On Aging,* 92d Cong., 2d sess., Part 3, August 9, 1972, p. 128.
3. *Ibid.*

SELECTED BIBLIOGRAPHY

ANDERSON, FERGUSEN W., *Practical Management of the Elderly,* pp. 41-48. Oxford, Great Britain: Blackwell Scientific Publication, 1967.

BERGMAN, ABRAHAM B., *Sudden Infant Death Syndrome.* Seattle, Washington: University of Washington Press, 1970.

"Biologist Says Science May Soon 'Cure' Death," *The Scrantonian* (Scranton, Pennsylvania), March 23, 1975, p. 13, col. 1.

FEIFEL, HERMAN, "Death," in *Taboo Topics*, ed. by Norman L. Farberow, p. 17. New York: Atherton Press, 1963.

GEERTINGER, PREBEN, *Sudden Death In Infancy*. Springfield, Illinois: Charles C. Thomas, 1968.

HELD, MARK L., "The Dying Child: The Importance of Understanding," *Medical Insight*, 6, no. 3 (March 1974), 12-19.

HENDIN, DAVID, *Death As a Fact of Life*, p. 115. New York: W.W. Norton & Company, Inc., 1973.

HORTON, LUCI, "The Mystery of Crib Death," *Ebony*, 28, no. 9 (July 1973), 58-62.

JACKSON, EDGAR, "Attitudes Toward Death in our Culture," in *Death and Bereavement*, ed. by A. H. Kutscher, p. 212. Springfield, Illinois: C.C. Thomas, 1969.

KASTENBAUM, ROBERT, "Death and Bereavement in Later Life," in *Death and Bereavement*, ed. A. H. Kutscher, p. 50. Springfield, Illinois: C.C. Thomas, 1969.

KOUPERNIK, ANTHONY, *The Child in his Family*. New York: John Wiley and Sons, 1973.

McGOUGH, ELIZABETH H., "Crib Death: Some Answers to 20,000 Sudden Tragedies," *Science Digest*, 67, no. 2 (February 1970), 26-30.

"Phone Service Comforts Dying or Proffers Advice to Grieving," *New York Times*, February 17, 1975, p. 22, col. 7.

PLANK, EMMA, "Death on a Children's Ward," *Medical Times*, 92, no. 7 (1964), 642-43.

RANDALL, OLLIE A., "Selecting a Nursing Home," in *The Care of the Geriatric Patient*, ed. by E.V. Cowdry, pp. 374-83. St. Louis, Missouri: C.V. Mosby Company, 1968.

U.S., Congress, Senate, *Hearings Before the Special Committee on Aging*, 92d Cong., 2d sess., August 9, 1972, pp. 127-135.

SULLIVAN, WALTER, "Can Scientists Someday Eliminate Old Age?" *Appleton-Neenah-Menasha Sunday Post Crescent* (Appleton, Wisconsin), November 9, 1975, sec. A, p. 6.

5

The Right to Die

Under the wide and starry sky,
Dig the grave and let me lie,
Glad did I live and gladly die,
And I laid me down with a will.
This be the verse you grave for me:
Here he lies where he longed to be;
Home is the sailor, home from the sea,
And the hunter home from the hill.

(ROBERT LOUIS STEVENSON "Requiem")

Euthanasia

We are well aware that people in almost all societies have a natural right to life as a consequence of being born. But, as a natural consequence of being born, do they also have a natural right to die? In his book, *The Forseeable Future*, Sir George Thomson suggests that once all causes of senility are conquered, death will either be accidental or intentional. Intentional death may be thought of in terms of euthanasia or suicide.

Before confronting the issue of euthanasia, we must define it. Historically, the definition was responsive to a single concept: allowing an easy or good death by promoting death for reasons of mercy. The word euthanasia actually comes from the Greek *eu*, meaning *well* and *thanatos*, meaning *death*. However, the total concept is not really so simply defined. There is 'promoting' death and then there is 'allowing' death. Where does one concern begin and the other leave off? It is this gray area that concerns many. The problem of understanding the total concept is further muddled by remembrances of Hitler and his infamous "euthanasia centers," in which it is estimated some 275 thousand people died. Hence, use of the term euthanasia reflects mass genocide in the minds of many.

Genocide may be defined as the deliberate and systematic destruction of a racial, political, or cultural group. Euthanasia, while deliberate, is not systematic. In fact, because of the possible analogy between genocide and euthanasia, many authorities have suggested the use of other terms such as orthothanasia, agathanasia, benomortasia, dysthanasia, antidysthanasia, or mercy killing. For purposes of communication throughout the remainder of this discussion, let us define euthanasia as the allowance of death through the removal or withholding of treatments that prolong life. (Another term for this is *indirect euthanasia*). Second, let us define an additional concern, mercy killing. In

68

mercy killing a deliberate action is taken causing death. This would include the administration of a fatal drug or an injection of air into the bloodstream that causes an air embolism resulting in death.

Further confusing the definitional game, for either of the above (euthanasia or mercy killing), we have to consider whether the patient is consciously choosing death or whether it is chosen for him while he is unconscious. Adding the terms voluntary and involuntary to the two previous terms may help clarify this confusion. Voluntary euthanasia can then be defined as the patient's granting of permission to allow for his death through removal or withholding of treatments that prolong life. Involuntary euthanasia implies the allowance of death *without* the patient's previous knowledge through removal or withholding of treatments that prolong life. Voluntary mercy killing can be described as the patient's granting of permission for deliberate action to be taken causing his death. Involuntary mercy killing can be described as a deliberate action taken without the patient's knowledge that hastens death. Indeed, some thin lines between the four definitions exist.

Looking at four examples of these definitions in practice may help alleviate any remaining confusion.

1. Mr. "X" asks his physician to remove him from the respirator if his condition worsens. (Voluntary Euthanasia)
2. Mr. "X" suddenly goes into a coma and is placed on the respirator. His relatives arrange to have him removed from the machine if his condition worsens. (Involuntary Euthanasia)
3. Mr. "X" asks his physician to administer a fatal drug if his condition worsens. (Voluntary Mercy Killing)
4. Mr. "X" suddenly goes into a coma. His family arranges for the physician to administer a fatal drug. (Involuntary Mercy Killing)

The concept of allowing or helping those in pain to die is founded in historical precedence. Trubo, in his research of euthanasia and mercy killing, found early use of the concept. On the Greek island of Cos, during the first century B.C., the old and the ill would gather at a banquet held once a year. There they would drink a poisonous chemical to promote death. Obviously, society as a whole, at that time, agreed with this practice. Furthermore, Trubo points out the following:

> A death potion was always kept in a public place in the Greek colony of Massila, to be used by those who could convince public officials that their death was justified. Aristotle advocated euthanasia for seriously deformed children. And Cicero wrote, "What reason is there for us to suffer? A door is open for us—death, eternal refuge where one is sensible of nothing.[1]

Using our definition, Aristotle was actually promoting mercy killing, but the point is that euthanasia and mercy killing are not concerns confronted only by modern society. Obviously, they have been considered as far back as recorded history demonstrates.

Apparently, the euthanasia issue was of sporadic concern around 1906, when the editor of *Independent* wrote:

> The renewal of interests in the old subject is due to the introduction of a bill into the Ohio Legislature providing that when an adult of sound mind has been fatally hurt or is so ill that recovery is impossible or is suffering extreme physical pain without hope of relief, his physician, if not a relative and if not interested in any way in the person's estate, may ask his patient in the presence of three witnesses if he or she is ready to die. If the answer is affirmative, then three other physicians are to be summoned in consultation, and if they agree that the case is hopeless, they are supposed to make arrangements to put the person out of pain and suffering with as little discomfort as possible.[2]

While the editor explains that the bill was supported by a distinguished scholar and humanitarian, he also remarks that civilization at that time would not consider such legislation seriously. Hindsight shows us that he was wrong. The bill was referred to a committee for further consideration by a vote of seventy-eight to twenty-two. This margin indicated an increasing number of advocates for euthanasia.

England, like the United States, was confronting the issue of euthanasia sporadically in the years to follow. In 1931, Dr. Milland, the newly elected President of the Society of Medical Officers of Health of England, gave a Presidential address advocating the legalization of voluntary mercy killing. He proposed that adults who were mentally competent and suffering from an incurable or fatal disease that might cause a slow and painful death should be allowed to substitute a quick and painless one. It was the opinion of the editor of the issue in which the President's Address appeared that the great majority of people of the western nations, at least, are not ready for such an innovation. In retrospect, it appears that he was wrong because various organizations supportive of euthanasia and mercy killing came into being shortly after this. While there are proponents of both euthanasia and mercy killing, as we have defined them, the former has gained the most support from various organizations. The first such organization was founded in England in 1935 under the name, the Voluntary Euthanasia Society.

Its American counterpart, the Euthanasia Society of America, was founded in 1938 by Reverend Charles Francis Potter. The Society was composed of lawyers, clergymen, doctors, and intellectuals who believed that the terminally ill had a 'right' to die with dignity. After many years and numerous unsuccessful attempts at legislation, members of the Society realized that a massive educational campaign was necessary. In 1967 members of the Euthanasia Society established the Euthanasia Educational Fund for just that purpose. This name was changed to the Euthanasia Educational Council in 1972. In 1975 The Euthanasia Society of America was reactivated under a changed name, The Society for the Right to Die, in order to help legislators introduce bills. Hence, at the present time, both the Society for the Right to Die and the Euthanasia Educational Council exist for the respective purposes of legislation and education. A major belief of the Euthanasia Educational Council is that each person should have the right to die with dignity. To attain this, they believe in education leading to understanding and acceptance of death with the end result being the discovery of ways to humanize death. Such ways include withdrawal of life-support techniques and machinery and the use of medication to eliminate pain, even if the medication tends to shorten life. However, proponents of euthanasia do not necessarily believe that drugs or other means should be used to directly promote death.

Various physicians oppose euthanasia on the grounds that it is contrary to the Oath of Hippocrates that all doctors must take. Others suggest that the Hippocratic Oath is outdated or easily misinterpreted. In 1948 the Hippocratic Oath was modified by the General Assembly of the World Medical Association. The following modification was later included in the International Code of Medical Ethics and was adopted in 1949 for subsequent use by physicians and medical schools:

> Declaration of Geneva: I solemnly pledge myself to consecrate my life to the service of humanity. I will give to my teachers the respect and gratitude which is their due; I will practice my profession with conscience and dignity; the health of my patient will be my first consideration; I will respect the secrets which are confided in me; I will maintain by all means in my power the honor and noble traditions of the medical profession. My colleagues will be my brothers; I will not permit considerations of religion, nationality, race, party politics, or social standing to intervene between my duty and my patient. I will maintain the utmost respect for human life from the time of conception; even under threat, I will not use my medical knowledge contrary to the laws of humanity. I make these promises solemnly, freely, and upon my honor.[3]

Notice, however, that the declaration does not support or denounce euthanasia *or* mercy killing. The question was not resolved by medical authorities at that time, and it remains unresolved even today.

Some nations, and even some states within the United States, have indicated movement toward legalization, or at least partial acceptance of euthanasia and mercy killing. Sweden allows voluntary euthanasia and voluntary mercy killing but not involuntary euthanasia or involuntary mercy killing. Hence, a physician can turn off or unplug life-sustaining machines but cannot administer a lethal poison. Interestingly though, he may place the poison in the hands of the patient for self-administration. Uruguay, extending the euthanasia concept of Sweden, allows mercy killing if it is administered as a result of patient request. The request is necessary to free the physician from any resulting prosecution. In such a case, the physician is said to have acted out of mercy and compassion. Norway's law is permissive because it is ambiguous. If a patient requests or consents to euthanasia and the physician heeds the request, the punishment is reduced below that outlined by Norweigian law. In effect, the physician is free from legal recourse. South Africa, in 1975, launched the South African Voluntary Euthanasia Society (S.A.V.E.S.). Their immediate goal is legislation of a euthanasia bill. Scottish law dictates that euthanasia is murder, however, no physician has ever been prosecuted for murder by euthanasia. English law, much like Scottish law, also considers euthanasia illegal. In fact, while permissiveness tends to be the rule, there appears to be no serious consideration of legalization. Rejected bills or motions in England include one proposed by the Voluntary Euthanasia Society in 1936, one discussed by the House of Lords and tabled before a vote was even taken in 1950, and one proposed by Lord Ragean of the House of Lords in 1969. Dignitaries and educators support, and have supported, these measures but they still fail to pass into English law. Regardless of legalization, a precedent for euthanasia was set in 1957:

> In 1957, a British Court found a doctor innocent of murder when he prescribed a pain-relieving drug which killed his patient. In that case, the jury was instructed by the presiding judge as follows: If the first purpose of medicine, the restoration of health, can no longer be achieved there is still much for a doctor to do, and he is entitled to do all that is proper and necessary to relieve pain and suffering, even if the measures he takes may incidently shorten human life.[4]

In the United States a movement toward legal reform also occurred. Defeated bills or motions regarding euthanasia include a 1937 Nebraska attempt, a 1947 New York attempt, and a 1968 state of Washington attempt. Of these, the most interesting defeat was the 1947 New York attempt. It began in 1945 with the Euthanasia Society sending letters to a group of physicians who had responded favorably to a Society poll. The letter asked each physician to join a medical committee for the legalization of euthanasia. Within a year, a committee of 1,776 physicians existed. A bill was drawn up that required the terminally ill patient to sign a petition for euthanasia and, along with an affidavit indicating terminal illness signed by his physician, the petition would be presented to a court of record. The court would appoint a three man commission of which two would be physicians. The commission would then investigate the case and present its finding to the court that would, in turn, make a final decision. Although support was obvious, the bill failed. Beginning in 1968, and each year thereafter, Dr. Walter W. Sackett Jr. has proposed a euthanasia bill in Florida. Dr. Sackett, a physician and member of the Florida House of Representatives, reported to a Special Committee on Aging that the United States should legalize the right to die when a person is irreversibly ill.

Since the Society for the Right to Die was reestablished out of the older Euthanasia Society of America in 1975, euthanasia bills have been introduced into the legislatures of at least fifteen states; among them are Oregon, Maryland, West Virginia, Idaho, Florida, Washington, Delaware, Wisconsin, Massachusetts, Illinois, Virginia, Rhode Island, Hawaii, and California. Legislators have noted increasing support for such a law in many of their states. In only one state, California, has such a bill been passed. Governor Brown signed into law, in October, 1976, a bill legalizing voluntary euthanasia. Referred to as a "right to die" bill, it allows any person, even those void of terminal illness at the time, to instruct the physician to cease life-support machines. Anyone in that state can sign a "living will," that must be witnessed by two people other than family members or the attending physician. (The "living will" concept will be discussed later in this chapter.) It remains in effect for a period of five years, and it may be renewed. Furthermore, it may be withdrawn at any time either verbally or in writing. In effect, physicians who comply with the living will and turn off or fail to use life-support devices may not be held liable for any crime or malpractice suit. Also, life insurance companies may not deny a person a policy because he or she has signed such a will.

No greater moral leader than Pope Pius XII has spoken on the issue at hand. In 1957, he asked "...does one have the right, or is one even under the obligation, to use modern artificial-respiration equipment in all cases, even those which, in the doctor's judgement, are completely hopeless?"[5] In answering his own questions, the Pope made it clear that the doctor reacts only to his patients' desires, either expressed or implied. As such, the physician should not provide care that is not desired by the patient or his guardian. Cardinal Villot, Vatican Secretary of State, summarized a letter to the International Federation of Catholic Medical Associations in 1970 indicating that medicine is at the service of man. Man, on the other hand, is not an instrument for medical science.

Quite a few doctors (probably unknowingly) support the statements made by Pope Pius XII and Cardinal Villot. Dr. Sackett has been quoted as saying that he has let hundreds of patients die. In fact, he claims that "...seventy-five percent of the doctors he has known did."[6] It is probably safe to assume that as a result of today's technological advances, many people can be kept "alive" almost indefinitely. It is also safe to assume that euthanasia, withdrawing treatments or machines and allowing death, is more common than might be suspected *or* admitted. It comes as no surprise that many physicians are afraid to exercise judgement or comply with a patient's desires if one examines the fantastic increase in malpractice suits. Dr. R. H. Williams of the University of Washington reported in a study that about eighty percent of a group of physicians and about eighty percent of a lay group favored euthanasia as we have defined it. Interestingly, about eighteen percent of the physicians and thirty-five percent of the lay group actually favored mercy killing as we have defined it. In the same year, Sanders reported that of 156 responding Chicago, Illinois internists and surgeons, sixty-one percent affirmed that euthanasia is practiced. This might indicate that law and medical practices are far apart in moralistic understanding. However, when the question comes to court, the gap separating law and medicine closes. On August 9, 1967, a twenty-three-year-old man killed his mother by shooting her in the head. He was subsequently charged with murder and brought to court. He explained to the court that his mother was in great pain, that she was suffering from leukemia, and that she had attempted suicide already. He further explained that she had begged him to kill her. So he did. The murder (voluntary mercy killing?) was premediated and intentional. The most lenient sentence he could legally be given was fourteen years in prison without probation. However, on January 24, 1969 he was found "Not Guilty" by reason of insanity. The jury also concluded that since he was no longer insane, he should be released. He was, and the case was ended.

Maguire, in his book, *Death By Choice*, offers a similar example in which a man was convicted of voluntary manslaughter for causing the death of his brother who was dying of cancer. He pleaded temporary insanity and claimed he was acting as a result of his brother's pleading. He was sentenced from three to five years in prison and fined five hundred dollars for his action.

On December 7, 1972 Dr. Vincent Montemarano allegedly injected a fatal overdose of potassium chloride into a cancer patient who had lapsed into a coma. On January 17, 1974 he was brought to trial. A licensed practical nurse maintained that Dr. Montemarano ordered her to fill a syringe with potassium chloride. She also testified that she saw the injection take place about ten minutes before the patient was pronounced dead. Dr. Anthony Di Beneditto, Chairman of the Department of Surgery where the alleged mercy killing took place, testified that Dr. Montemarano confessed that he had given a dying patient potassium chloride to stop his heart. The defense never accepted the premise that an injection was made. In fact, both sides avoided reference to 'mercy killing.' Regardless, it was suggested by one newspaper reporter that many individuals believed it was a case of mercy killing. Over a hundred people in the courtroom and hundreds more waiting outside the courtroom awaited the verdict. As it was announced that Dr. Montemarano was not guilty, those in the courtroom broke into a loud and prolonged applause. This may be another indication of increasing attitudinal acceptance toward euthanasia and mercy killing.

In summarizing the preceding examples and the California bill, it can be said that, in general, the attitudes of people toward euthanasia *are* changing. In a 1973 survey regarding attitudes toward death, Dr. John W. Riley Jr., of the Office of Social Research of the Equitable Life Assurance Society, reported that only twenty-six percent of his national sample expressed the belief that doctors should use any means possible for keeping a patient alive. A more recent California poll suggested that almost nine out of every ten Californians polled believe that a terminal patient should have the right to refuse life-prolonging medication. Perhaps surprisingly, sixty-three percent support the right of an incurable patient to ask for and receive medication that would end his life.

Perhaps the time for reexamination of euthanasia and mercy killing is approaching. On April 15, 1975 twenty-one-year-old Karen Ann Quinlan lapsed into a coma. Breathing had stopped and artificial respiration techniques were employed to keep her alive until she reached a hospital. Although the cause of cessation of breathing had not been determined, interruption in the normal breathing process apparently caused anoxia (an insufficient supply of oxygen to parts of the body), resulting in a coma. She was placed on a respirator for assistance in breathing, at which time her own breathing did not resume. She remained on the respirator, in what her physician called an altered level of consciousness. Dr. Robert Morse, a neurologist in charge of her care, maintained that Karen Quinlan was not brain-dead. He referred to the Ad Hoc Committee of Harvard Medical School Criteria as the ordinary medical standard for determining brain death. Karen Ann Quinlan satisfied none of these criteria. She reportedly did not have a completely flat EEG, and she did exhibit involuntary muscle activity.

After three and a half months on the life-sustaining machine, Karen had not progressed. The original cause of her condition was still unknown. Her parents argued that the young woman was not really alive. Karen's parents consulted Father Trapasso, their family priest, and they were informed of the Roman Catholic Church's position of not using extraordinary means to sustain life. With the Father's support, Karen's parents asked the physician to discontinue all extraordinary measures. Dr. Morse refused indicating that his moral conscience would not allow him to agree to the cessation of the respirator.

On September 13, 1975, nearly five months after Karen went into a coma and was placed on the respirator, Mr. and Mrs. Quinlan filed a court action to have the machine unplugged. Her parents, religious in nature, claimed that it was God's will that their daughter be allowed to die. Their belief was that Karen was already dead and that it was only the machine that was keeping her alive. The legal papers filed by their attorney, Paul W. Armstrong, quoted doctors who had determined that Miss Quinlan suffered irreparable brain damage during her five months in a coma.

However, permission from the court to discontinue use of the machine was denied. On November 10, 1975 Judge Robert Muir, Jr. refused to allow the removal of the respirator that was keeping Karen Ann Quinlan alive. Legally and medically, Karen Ann Quinlan was still alive at that time. Alive also is the issue; who has the right, if anyone, to terminate life? Should euthanasia, either expressed or implied, be subject to legal control? The case continued. On December 17, 1975 the Quinlans were in the process of taking the case to the New Jersey Supreme Court. A hearing was scheduled for January 26, 1976. Some additional concerns came out of the Quinlan case at that time. Reacting to the court's decision of November 10, 1975, numerous religious and medical authorities made statements. Most of them supported the Judge's decision. However, Reverend William B. Smith, representing the Roman Catholic Archdiocese of New York, believed that the trusted judgement of medical authorities should be preferred to any legal decision. Dr. Max H. Parrot from Portland, Oregon commented that Judge Muir "recognized that such decisions are essentially medical rather than legal, and therefore the care and treatment of a patient and all decisions related thereto remain the responsibility of the treating physician."[7] Perhaps the most important reaction to the Quinlan court case came from Ralph Porzio, the lawyer for the doctors involved. He requested an international conference of the best medical and legal minds available to sit down and organize guidelines for solving future problems like those raised by the Quinlan case.

On March 31, 1976 the New Jersey Supreme Court ruled 7–0 in favor of allowing the removal of the respirator that had kept Karen Ann Quinlan alive for almost a year. Chief Justice Richard J. Hughes stipulated that doctors and a hospital ethics committee must agree that there was no reasonable possibility of her recovery before removal would be allowed. Once such an agreement was reached, criminal charges against the hospital or doctors would not be possible. Karen's father was appointed her personal guardian by the court. This meant that if the original doctors at the hospital did not agree with removal of the respirator, he had the power to choose other doctors who would make the decision. However, the hospital ethics committee still had to agree with the doctors before removal was allowed. Neither the former court-appointed guardian nor the New Jersey attorney general appealed the Supreme Court decision.

Almost two months later, on May 24, 1976, Karen Ann Quinlan was moved to a private room where the respirator was removed. It was believed she would die almost immediately. She did not. While still in a coma, Miss Quinlan continued to breath on her own. There is, at this time, still no sign of recovery from her long coma. Most medical experts agree that she has probably suffered irreversible brain damage and could remain in a vegetative state indefinitely.

On June 10, 1976 Karen was moved to a nursing home where "extraordinary medical treatment" to keep her alive will not be used. It is unclear to this day what is meant by "extraordinary medical treatment."

Most people who argue against euthanasia suggest at one point or another that the physician can never be sure of what tomorrow's medicine may bring. What if the day after he lets Tommy die, a cure for cancer is found? What if the day after the court allowed Quinlan's respirator to be removed, a cure for "irreversible brain damage" was found? The question is one that can never be answered satisfactorily, mainly because these are rare cases. There are cases of those painfully dying from terminal cancer who, for no apparent reason, recover to outlive their doctors. Prognosis is fallible and diseases may go into unaccountable remission for no apparent reason. Yet, the percentages are behind the practice of medicine. Prognosis of some diseases or disorders can be very precise. However, the reality of the situation is that there *are* those cases where life is present but hope is not.

Randal Carmen, age seventeen, was kept alive on life-support machines for three weeks before he died. According to doctors, Randal spent three weeks on machines after his brain was dead. Repeated requests by his parents to end his life by removing the machines were ignored. The doctor maintained that everything within medical power must be done to maintain life saving procedures. Other than the prospect of life, should one not consider the excruciating pain that sometimes accompanies death? Should one not consider the dignity of the "person," or is his dignity secondary to the very technology that keeps him alive? Are physical signs of life more important than emotional or spiritual concerns? Do we keep the "body" alive at any cost? (For example, the estimated cost for keeping Karen Ann Quinlan alive for five months from April 15, 1975 to September 21, 1975 was one hundred thirty thousand dollars.) These are all questions that remain unanswered by medical or legal authorities. Yet each individual may have to confront them at some point in his life.

A second argument against euthanasia is that neither physicians nor courts have the right to "play God." This argument can no longer be taken seriously in today's advanced medical-technological world. If it is God's will that we are concerned with, then medicine should be abolished to allow God's work to continue. If it is wrong to promote death and to put an end to suffering, likewise, it is wrong to delay death with medication or respirators. Very few people would abandon the advances that medical technology has made over the last few decades.

Recently, the movement toward 'Death with Dignity' has intensified. During the 1970s, at least fifteen euthanasia bills have been introduced in various states; one passed. Over seventy thousand members have enlisted support for the Euthanasia Educational Council. In 1967, Luis Kutner suggested a 'Living Will' to the Euthanasia Educational Fund (now the Euthanasia Educational Council). Such wills have little legal foundation (except in California); however, there were one million of these wills distributed as of March 1976. While it is a legal document, it has not yet been tested in a court of law. It must be signed in the presence of two witnesses but does not have to be notarized. A copy should be kept on hand at all times. It is even recommended that copies be given to your doctor and next of kin so that your wishes are known. A copy of the document as it is today is shown on page 79.

It remains to be seen if these documents will be medically honored or if the courts will support the doctor's decision (other than in California where its use is legalized). Interestingly, courts are not usually called upon to support a doctor in his selection of which treatment is applicable to the patient. Whereas one treatment may cause a shorter but happier life, another may result in a longer, but more pain-filled life. The doctor makes these moral decisions everyday. To remove this power of moral decision making from the physician is to assume that all of us want to live as long as possible regardless of the pain or circumstances. While many of us may want this, there are also many, if not more, who do not. This is evidenced by the advancement of the euthanasia movement in the United States and in other countries.

Just a few years ago, a 'Patient's Bill of Rights' was approved by the American Hospital Association. It maintained that every patient had twelve basic rights. Among those pertaining to various aspects of euthanasia were:

TO MY FAMILY, MY PHYSICIAN, MY LAWYER, MY CLERGYMAN

TO ANY MEDICAL FACILITY IN WHOSE CARE I HAPPEN TO BE

TO ANY INDIVIDUAL WHO MAY BECOME RESPONSIBLE FOR MY HEALTH, WELFARE OR AFFAIRS

Death is as much a reality as birth, growth, maturity and old age—it is the one certainty of life. If the time comes when I, _____ can no longer take part in decisions for my own future, let this statement stand as an expression of my wishes, while I am still of sound mind.

If the situation should arise in which there is no reasonable expectation of my recovery from physical or mental disability, I request that I be allowed to die and not be kept alive by artificial means or "heroic measures". I do not fear death itself as much as the indignities of deterioration, dependence and hopeless pain. I, therefore, ask that medication be mercifully administered to me to alleviate suffering even though this may hasten the moment of death.

This request is made after careful consideration. I hope you who care for me will feel morally bound to follow its mandate. I recognize that this appears to place a heavy responsibility upon you, but it is with the intention of relieving you of such responsibility and of placing it upon myself in accordance with my strong convictions, that this statement is made.

Signed _____

Date _____

Witness _____

Witness _____

Copies of this request have been given to _____

_____

_____

_____

A Living Will[8]

1. The right to information concerning diagnosis, treatment, and prognosis
2. The right to advance information prior to consent for surgery or any other type of treatment
3. The right to refuse treatment

The third right listed above is extremely important for proponents of legalized euthanasia. The American Hospital Association claims that eighty-five percent of the nation's hospitals have accepted the Bill in principle; however, only thirty-five percent have used it in any form. Many people feel that the Bill should either be posted where all can see it, or that it should be given to each patient as he enters the hospital.

As we will look at various religious attitudes regarding euthanasia in a later chapter, let us summarize the situation up to this point. About forty-two percent of the religions mentioned in the next chapter accept euthanasia as an individual decision to be made between the doctor, the patient, and the family. Slightly less (about thirty-five percent) are acceptant of mercy killing, usually depending upon the circumstances.

Summarily, we can suggest support for euthanasia for the following reasons:

1. To alleviate pain and suffering
2. To promote "meaning" to the state of life
3. Economic considerations
4. Use of hospital bed space, staff, and technological devices (that could be used by others)

While the last two reasons may not add much to the concept of "death with dignity," they are realistic concerns and must not be overlooked in any discussion for or against the practice of euthanasia. Likewise, there are reasons against euthanasia that are equally founded in logic. Those who oppose euthanasia usually do so citing the following:

1. The Oath of Hippocrates
2. Moral decision making by physicians and family
3. Religious considerations

Suicide

From this world-wearied flesh. Eyes, look your last!
Arms, take your last embrace! and, lips, O you
The doors of breath, seal with a righteous kiss
A dateless bargain to engrossing death!
Come, bitter conduct, come, unsavory guide!
Thou desperate pilot, now at once run on
The dashing rocks they sea-sick weary bark!
Here's to my love! O true apothecary!
Thy drugs are quick. Thus with a kiss I die.

(WILLIAM SHAKESPEARE Romeo and Juliet, Act V, Scene 3)

Again we have to ask if any individual has the right to take his own life. The law of any country allows killing as a legitimate activity depending upon circumstances. It may be acceptable to kill the enemy in a war; however, it is not acceptable to kill the "enemy" next door. It may also be acceptable to kill a convicted murderer; but again, not acceptable for the murderer to kill. This is all to say that in some cases the manner of death may be considered legitimate and socially and morally acceptable. Suicide, however, is rarely an acceptable form of dying.

In the United States, suicide is regarded as a crime under common law. Traditionally, anyone who attempted suicide and failed was placed in jail. In rare cases, some were sentenced to the death penality. Obviously, if one succeeded in suicide, he also succeeded in avoiding legal prosecution. Recently, however, legal sanctions have tended to do away with this law and to replace it with an extensive attempt to treat attempted suicides as emotional or "mental" cases. Although suicide is still a crime in eight states, every state in the United States provides mandatory psychiatric hospitalization for attempted suicides from a minimum of three to fifteen days with an option for renewal. If the individual is diagnosed as mentally incompetent, psychiatric hospitalization is extended.

In 1961 England passed a Suicide Act that implied that it was not illegal to attempt suicide, regardless of the circumstances. However, it is still illegal for anyone to assist a person in doing so. This act is indicative of a change in attitudes toward suicide.

Traditionally, western culture developed its attitudes toward suicide from other cultures and religions. Early Christians believed that suicide was worse than any other crime. Strict Christians still adhere to the arguments against suicide that St. Thomas Aquinas proposed. He maintained that:

1. Self-destruction is contrary to man's natural inclinations, natural law, and the charity a man owed himself.
2. Man has no right to deprive society of his presence and activity by suicide.
3. Since we are God's property, it is for God to decide on our lives and deaths.

While the reasons for suicide vary, sociologist Emile Durkheim described three distinct types of suicides:

1. Altruistic—A person sacrifices himself for a "greater good"
2. Anomic—Sudden normlessness; group standards suddenly no longer seem to apply
3. Egoistic—An individual lacks strong group or social ties

Altruistic suicide is often associated with the history of the development of a nation. Such an example might be the soldier who jumps on a hand grenade so that others may live. This can be identified as the "hara-kiri" approach. Let us now look at this approach since it is the most recent example of mass suicide for the ultimate good of a nation. Hara-kiri was widely practiced by the Japanese during the Second World War.

The word *hara*, or abdomen, has a common root with the word *hari*, which means tension. The ancient Japanese associated tension in the abdomen with the soul since it was believed that the abdomen was the place where the soul resided. Literally, *hara-kiri* means *belly-cutting* or *suicide by disembowelment*. The word, though widely known abroad, is rarely used by the Japanese who call it *seppuki*. This custom of suicide arose during the days when self-inflicted death was preferable to capture and mutilation by a merciless enemy. It was fostered by the knight's code, which taught that death was better than disgrace.

Hara-kiri was widely practiced by men of the *samurai*, the military class in feudal Japan. It was practiced if the samurai believed he had failed in his duty or if he was faced with the need to surrender. If the samurai had been found guilty of a crime, it was also regarded as a privilege to die in this manner rather than at the hands of an executioner.

Men who worked for the lords became the warrior caste, the samurai. These men followed a code of behavior that relates to some of the behavior affecting the Japanese even today. The samurai's sole ambition was to obey his lord, to die fighting in his service, and if necessary, to avenge his lord's death. Death in battle was glorified, especially when it occurred while obeying the call of duty.

There are two distinct types of hara-kiri, voluntary and obligatory. Voluntary hara-kiri evolved during the wars of the twelfth century as a method of suicide used frequently by warriors who, defeated in battle, chose to avoid the dishonor of falling into the hands of the enemy. Obligatory hara-kiri was a method of capital punishment used by the samurai in order that they be spared the disgrace of being beheaded by a common executioner. This practice was common until 1873 when it was finally abolished. Hara-kiri, an extremely painful and slow means of suicide, was favored as an effective way to demonstrate the courage, self-control, and strong resolve of the samurai. Hence, voluntary hara-kiri, as atonement for defeat or as self-sacrifice, was highly praised and occurs occasionally even today. From this, one might conclude that all suicides are not necessarily "insane" acts. Hara-kiri represents that class of suicide that is seemingly rational in nature. There are individual cases of suicide, apart from hara-kiri, that have been just as rational in nature.

At this point it should be mentioned that Durkheim, in a footnote, suggested that there might be a fourth type of suicide, which he labeled "fatalistic." Defined as "...suicide driving from excessive regulation, that of persons with futures pitilessly blocked and passions violently choked by oppressive discipline,"[9] it appears as though this type might be more prevalent today than when Durkheim set up his three types. Regardless, suicide in the United States is generally of an egoistic or anomic type. Statistically, for all ages, suicide is ranked eleventh as a cause of death; however, the exact number of suicides is not really known. Experts estimate that between twenty-five and sixty thousand people succeed each year. An additional two hundred thousand attempt suicide and fail. Depending on the source, these estimates vary. The general suicide rate is at the same level now as it was at the beginning of the century. This indicates that the suicide rate is not rising steadily as many believe it is. Confusing the issue of suicide statistics is the belief that many accidents are suicides. They are often disguised as accidents so that insurance companies cannot avoid the insurance payments. Additionally, suicide is an equal-opportunity employer; all socio-economic classes contribute to the suicide rate. It is not always the poor or the underprivileged who commit suicide. Professionals and children who have everything they could possibly want also take their own lives. In fact, cases of suicide are more common among privileged groups in our society than among those generally considered "lower class." To break another myth surrounding this phenomenon, suicide is not an inherited trait, although there are families with a history of suicides. Apparently, there may be a hereditary predisposition to react in a certain manner; however, there is no evidence of suicidal tendencies being linked to hereditary traits as such.

It has been estimated that approximately two-thirds of all those who attempt suicide do not really wish to die; they are calling out for help. Additionally, about thirty percent are ambivalent about their wishes. Only about three to five percent are actually determined to commit suicide. In a study of 742 suicides, only twenty-four percent left notes. The notes were analyzed and it was proposed that fifty-one percent had what was termed positive content, six percent had negative content, twenty-five percent had neutral content, and eighteen percent had mixed emotional content.

Warning signals or suicide threats can be verbally direct or indirect. About sixty percent voice direct threats, while twenty percent voice indirect threats. Warning signals can also be exemplified through personal behavior. Such things as previous attempts, insomnia, a neglect of personal appearance, outward signs of depression, and/or giving away valued possessions are all indicators of possible suicidal tendencies. About three-quarters of those who commit suicide have talked about it beforehand; a great majority of those have even given advance notice.

Among adolescents, suicide is the third leading cause of death. Most adolescents use reversible methods like sleeping pills, aspirin, or wrist slitting. This appears to indicate that they wish to be stopped. However, for those adolescents who do use irreversible methods, males tend to do so more often than females. Such irreversible methods include shooting, hanging, or jumping from bridges and buildings.

Suicide ranks second as a leading cause of death among college-age students. Females outnumber males in attempted suicides; however, males outnumber females in success by a ratio of about two to one. Compared to noncollege people of the same age group, twice as many college-enrolled students take their lives. This rate is higher among first semester freshmen and first semester graduate students. The methods used are similar to those used by adolescents.

It should be noted that suicide is not only an adolescent or college-age problem. People over sixty-five account for a good proportion of all suicides. Determining factors leading to suicide in the aged include depression, unemployment, retirement, financial worries, mental illness, senility, physical illness, loneliness, the threat of becoming an invalid, and the death of a spouse or someone close. Apparently, everything that comes with old age (but does not have to) predisposes suicide. Emphasis on youth and the youth culture has much to do with the elderly person's feelings. Also, emphasis on success has taken children away from parents, often causing depression among them.

Most of the aged prevent suicidal feelings through social involvement or by keeping close family ties. This helps them avoid depression and preserves their mental health. Dr. Dan Leviton, professor of Health Education at the University of Maryland, suggests that sexual activity among the aged may act as a deterrent to suicide. Leviton maintains that where sexuality among the elderly is strong, the desire for death, especially by suicide, is weak. Of course, it is not actually sexual interaction that prevents suicide. Rather, it is the whole concept of living a meaningful life that enters the picture. There is, for some reason, a general myth that sexual activity after sixty years of age must decline. This myth should vanish, and sexual activity among the elderly should be accepted. Leviton suggests the availability of pornographic materials and legal prostitution to legitimize sexuality among the aged. Thus, the aged might be able to continue their lives in a meaningful sense, in spite of the social role-playing that they are forced into.

Sometimes, however, pain in life is worse than the thought of death. A Gallup poll conducted between April 4th and 7th of 1975 indicated increasing support of this concept. While forty-one percent of the American people surveyed believe it is not wrong to commit suicide if the person involved is in great pain with no hope for improvement, fifty-one percent believe the opposite. These percentages reveal an increase in moral acceptance of suicide over other studies of previous years.

Putting this concept into practice, Dr. Henry Pitney Van Dusen, seventy-seven years old and a former president of the Union Theological Seminary, and his wife, Elizabeth, age eighty, took an overdose of sleeping pills. Mrs. Van Dusen left the following letter:

> To all Friends and Relations,
>
> We hope that you will understand what we have done even though some of you will disapprove of it and some be disillusioned by it.
>
> We have both had very full and satisfying lives.
>
> Pitney has worked hard and with great dedication for the church. *I* have had an adventurous and happy life. We have both had happy lives, and our children have crowned this happiness.
>
> But since Pitney had his stroke five years ago, we have not been able to do any of the things we want to do and *are* able to do, and my arthritis is much worse.
>
> There are too many helpless old people who without modern medicinal care would have died, and we feel God would have allowed them to die when their time had come.
>
> Nowadays it is difficult to die. We feel that this way we are taking will become more usual and acceptable as the years pass.
>
> Of course the thought of our children and our grandchildren *make* us sad, but we still feel that this is the best way and the right way to go. We are both increasingly weak and unwell and who would want to die in a Nursing Home.
>
> We are not afraid to die.
>
> We send you all our love and gratitude for your wonderful support and friendship.
>
> "O Lamb of God that takest away the sins of the world
> Have mercy upon us
> O Lamb of God that takest away the sins of the world
> Grant us thy peace."

Mrs. Van Dusen died within hours. Dr. Van Dusen survived, but died of a heart attack fifteen days later. Judge for yourself whether or not the Van Dusens were mentally competent and whether or not they had the right to take their lives.

Psychiatrists and religious authorities disagree amongst themselves regarding this alleged right. At the Eighth International Congress on Suicide Prevention, held in Jerusalem in October of 1975, more than five hundred psychiatrists from twenty-one nations assembled to hear more than one hundred presentations on suicide. Dr. Seymour Perlin of George Washington University maintained that the best life is not necessarily the longest. It depends on what is right and good for the individual. Dr. Uri Lovrental, from Israel, suggested that human life is unique and must be maintained at almost any cost. He agreed, however, that human dignity sometimes takes precedence over life. Justice Chaim Cohen, Chief Justice of the Israeli Supreme Court, contended that suicide is permissible in Judaism to avoid death by slow torture. However, a Roman Catholic priest, a Protestant minister, and an Islamic scholar at the Congress maintained that any suicide is inexcusable and unpardonable. They did attempt to make a distinction between suicide and martyrdom. At any rate, there is disagreement among psychiatrists and religious authorities. Almost all reached the agreement, however, that suicide prevention is a worthwhile endeavor.

Recently, a mass of suicide prevention centers have been established adding their numbers to the four that had existed for years. Nearly two hundred suicide prevention centers now exist in the United States. Centers are established by Universities, Churches, and various other nonprofit groups. Are they busy? Each year, over six thousand people call Save-A-Life, a New York Center; ten thousand call the Los Angeles Suicide Prevention Center; and, twenty thousand call the San Francisco Suicide Prevention Center. Yes, the Suicide Prevention Centers in the United States are busy.

What are they? What do they do? Most of them are places where those who are considering suicide can call for help and talk to someone who cares. The three to five percent who are intent on committing suicide are going to do so regardless of help, but the other ninety-five to ninety-seven percent may be helped. Their concern is to try to reach those who are confused, i.e., those who do not really know if they want to die or those who *want* to be talked out of it.

Employees at suicide prevention centers are trained to help those calling. They generally go through a series of five steps:

1. Establish a relationship, maintain contact, and obtain information
2. Identify and clarify the focal problem
3. Evaluate the suicide potential
4. Assess the individual's strengths and resources
5. Formulate a constructive plan and mobilize the individual's resources

Evaluating the suicide potential is done by using a preestablished formula including such variables as:[10]

1. Age: Considered high-risk are those forty-five years and older. Considered low risk are those under forty-five years of age.
2. Sex: Considered high-risk are males. Considered low-risk are females.
3. Race: Considered high-risk are whites. Considered low-risk are nonwhites.
4. Marital Status: Considered high-risk are those separated, divorced, or widowed. Considered low-risk are single or married people.
5. Employment Status: Considered high-risk are the unemployed or retired. Considered low-risk are the employed.
6. Living Arrangements: Considered high-risk are those living alone. Considered low-risk are those living with others.
7. Health: Considered high-risk are those suffering from poor health. Considered low-risk are those in good health.
8. Mental Condition: Considered high-risk are those who have previously had a mental or emotional disorder, including alcoholism. Considered low-risk are those who are presumably normal.
9. Method: Considered high-risk are those who wish to use guns, hanging, jumping, or drowning. Considered low-risk are those who wish to use cutting, carbon monoxide, or a combination or methods.
10. Previous Attempt or Threat: Considered high-risk are those who have attempted or threatened before. Considered low-risk are those who have not.

While other variables may be included, the above are agreed upon by authorities in the field of suicide prevention. Hence, if you are considering suicide and happen to be a white male over forty-five years of age, separated from your wife, unemployed or retired, living alone in poor physical and mental health (perhaps alcoholic), and you have threatened to attempt suicide before, you should seek immediate help. You may not even know it, but chances are, according to the risk factors, that you will succeed in your attempt.

With the development of suicide prevention programs, unnecessary suicides can be avoided. By now you have probably realized that the issue of the morality of suicide has been avoided. This has been done purposely. Whether or not one has a "right" to take his own life is a question that you must ask yourself. Legally, change regarding punishment for attempted suicide has been made in England and the United States. Morally, some change has also taken place. Rarely is society concerned with suicide as an act or a crime; rather, it is concerned with the person who attempts or commits it. For example, on October 5, 1975 the Riverside County District Attorney of Palm Springs, California maintained that no charges be brought against William Plachta who stood by while his wife committed suicide. The official, Byron Morton, suggested that Mr. Plachta *acted out of love and compassion* for his terminally ill wife. The right to die appears to be gaining as much support as the right to live has always had.

SUMMARY

The right to die involves four separate concerns including voluntary and involuntary mercy killing and voluntary and involuntary euthanasia. None of the four are new *concerns because all of these have existed in the past.*

At the present time, some countries have legalized voluntary euthanasia or have decreased the criminal penality to such an extent that fear of prosecution is minimal. Various organizations in the United States, as well as in other countries, support legislative and educational programs for voluntary euthanasia. However, only California has legalized such a concern.

Rationale supportive of voluntary euthanasia is based on relatively new medical technology that enables the physician to maintain "life" for extended periods of time after clinical death has occurred. The Karen Ann Quinlan case is only one example that demonstrates the extent to which the medical-technological-institutional complex will go in order to maintain life.

We can identify four types of (or reasons for) suicide: altrustic, anomic, egoistic, and fatalistic. Generally, however, warning signals or suicide threats precede a suicide attempt.

While suicide is the third leading cause of death among adolescents, it is interesting to note that females tend to use reversible methods, i.e., methods that give a potential rescuer a greater probability of succeeding in saving her life. Males, on the other hand, tend to use irreversible methods.

Suicide can be a well thought out, rational act. It is not always *the result of an emotional imbalance. England realized this when they enacted legislation making it legal to commit suicide. It is, however, illegal for anyone to assist the attempt.*

Suicide prevention centers have been established in many parts of the United States. These organizations attempt to gain information from the potential suicide victim. This information correlates with a number of personal factors or variables that, when combined, indicate the suicide potential of the possible victim.

1. Richard Trubo, *An Act of Mercy* (Los Angeles: Nash Publishing, 1973), p. 5.

2. "Euthanasia Once More," *Independent*, 60 (February 1, 1906), 291.

3. G. E. W. Wolsten Holme and Maeve O'Connor, *Ethics In Medical Progress* (Boston: Little, Brown and Co., 1966), p. 222.

4. Trubo, *An Act of Mercy*, p. 37.

5. U.S., Congress, Senate, *Hearings Before The Special Committee On Aging*, 92d Cong., 2d sess., p. 149.

6. *Ibid.*, p. 148.

7. Peter Kihss, "Religious and Medical Leaders Back Court's Decision In The Quinlan Case," *New York Times*, November 11, 1975, p. 62, col. 1.

8. Reprinted with permission of the Euthanasia Educational Council, 250 West 57th Street, New York, New York 10019.

9. Emile Durkheim, *Suicide*, trans. by John A. Spaulding and George Simpson (New York: The Free Press, 1951), p. 276.

10. H. L. P. Resnik, *Suicidal Behavior* (Boston: Little, Brown and Company, 1968), p. 196.

SELECTED BIBLIOGRAPHY

DURKHEIM, EMILE, *Suicide: Prevention and Intervention*. Boston: Beacon Press, 1951.

EPSTEIN, HELEN, "A Sin Or A Right?" *New York Times*, September 8, 1974, sec. 6, p. 91.

EUTHANASIA EDUCATIONAL COUNCIL, *Euthanasia*. New York: December 1974.

EUTHANASIA EDUCATIONAL COUNCIL, *Euthanasia: An Annotated Bibliography*. New York: June 1974.

EUTHANASIA EDUCATIONAL COUNCIL, *"In Her Own Words."* New York.

EUTHANASIA EDUCATIONAL COUNCIL, *Euthanasia News*. New York. Vol. 1, no. 3 (May 1975); Vol. 1, no. 3 (August 1975); Vol. 1, no. 4 (November 1975).

"Euthanasia Once More," *Independent*, 60 (February 1, 1906), 291–292.

"Excerpts From Judge Muir's Decision in the Karen Quinlan Case," *New York Times*, November 11, 1975, p. 62, col. 4.

"God's Will Be Done, Father Says in Suit to Let Girl Die," *Milwaukee Sentinal*, September 17, 1975, p. 1, col. 3.

HENRY, ANDREW F. AND JAMES F. SHORT JR., "The Sociology of Suicide," in *Clues to Suicide*, ed. by Edwin S. Shneidman and Norman L. Farberow, p. 60. New York: McGraw-Hill Book Company, Inc., 1957.

HOLME, WOLSTEN G. E. W. AND MAEVE O'CONNOR, *Ethics in Medical Progress*, p. 222. Boston: Little, Brown and Co., 1966.

ILLSON, MURRAY, "Court Orders Doctors to Feed a Woman Who Wants to Die," *New York Times*, October 25, 1975, p. 33, col. 4.

KIHSS, PETER, "Religious and Medical Leaders Back Court's Decision in the Quinlan Case," *New York Times*, November 11, 1975, p. 62, col. 1.

LORD, CHRISTINA, "Issues in Quinlan Case Divide Clerics in Rome," *New York Times*, October 25, 1975, pp. 1, 33.

MAGUIRE, DANIEL C., *Death by Choice*, pp. 25, 132, 148. New York: Doubleday and Company, Inc., 1974.

"Mercy Killing Trial Opens Tomorrow," *New York Times*, January 13, 1974, sec. 1, p. 44, col. 4.

"New Jersey Case Raises Issue of When Life Ends," *New York Times*, September 21, 1975, sec. 4, p. 7, col. 1.

RESNIK, H. L. P., *Suicidal Behavior*, pp. 49, 196. Boston: Little, Brown and Company, 1968.

SANDERS, JOSEPH, "Euthanasia: None Dare Call It Murder," *Journal of Criminal Law, Criminology, and Police Science*, 60, no. 3 (1969), 351.

"Shall We Legalize Homicide," *Outlook*, 82 (February 3, 1906), 252.

SILVER, RAY R., "Key Moments in L.I. Trial," *New York Times*, February 10, 1974, sec. 1, p. 98, col. 3.

SILVER, RAY R., "Physician Acquitted in Patient's Death," *New York Times*, February 6, 1974, pp. 1, 44.

SMITH, TERENCE, "Suicide Debated by Psychiatrists," *New York Times*, October 26, 1975, sec. 1, p. 68, col. 1.

SULLIVAN, JOSEPH E., "Judge Rules Out Removal of the Quinlan Respirator," *New York Times*, November 11, 1975, pp. 1, 62.

THOMSON, GEORGE, *The Foreseeable Future*. London: Cambridge University Press, 1960.

Trubo, Richard, *An Act Of Mercy*, pp. 5, 36, 37, 46–48. Los Angeles: Nash Publishing, 1973.

U.S., Congress, Senate, *Hearings Before The Special Committee On Aging*, 92d Cong., 2d sess., August 9, 1972, pp. 147–50.

"Voluntary Euthanasia," *American Journal of Public Health*, 22 (February 1932), 180–182.

Williams, R. H., *To Live and to Die*, pp. 90–91. New York: Springer-Verlag New York Inc., 1973.

"Youth Kept Alive 3 Weeks Is Dead," *New York Times*, October 12, 1975, sec. 1, p. 51, col. 1.

6

Burial Customs

"Bury me," the bishop said,
"Close to my geranium bed;
Lay me near the gentle birch.
It is lonely in the church,
And its vaults are damp and chill!
Noble men sleep there, but still
House me in the friendly grass!
Let the linnets sing my mass!"

Dying Swithin had his whim
And the green sod covered him.

(DANIET HENDERSON "ST. SWITHIN")

Cultural and Religious Concerns

The attitudes and beliefs held by past and present religions and cultures strongly influence the procedures employed just prior to, during, and after death. These procedures, utilized for centuries, can best be defined as customs. Such customs include rituals before death (when death is certain), rituals observed once death has occurred, and funeral procedures including both the viewing and the burial. Customs of past religions and cultures can at least partially be identified in present religions and cultures. As we discuss some past cultural customs, try to identify those that remain in our culture today.

Among the lower class, economically deprived Egyptians of the past, funerals were very much like ours with respect to embalming and burial. However, other aspects were quite different. Throughout the mourning process, the family would cover their faces with mud. The body would then be taken to the embalmers, embalmed, and placed in a casket. The few personal ornaments that a person might have collected throughout his life were placed alongside of him. Sandles were placed on his feet, and a staff, to support his steps as he made the long journey into the next world, was placed next to him in the casket. He was buried in a hole, a cave, or in the sand of the open desert and left.

The funeral of a king, member of the royal family, or a very rich person in Egypt was quite different, as different as it is today between upper and lower socioeconomic classes. During a king's funeral, the people of the country would weep and tear their clothing. All of the temples would close and all celebrations or festivals would cease for a seventy-two day period. It was said to take this long to prepare the king's body for the journey into the next world. Crowds of two to three

93

hundred men and women would walk around the streets with mud on their heads and their garments knotted around their bodies. They would sing songs daily, not eat wheat or meat, and not drink wine or indulge themselves in luxuries of any kind. The seventy-two days were spent in grief and mourning. Meanwhile, the funeral preparations were made, and on the last day of mourning, the body was placed in a coffin and laid at the entrance of the king's tomb. Also on the last day, the people judged the acts of the king during his lifetime. The casket was then taken and placed on a boat and sailed across the nearest river. If the king was decidedly bad, by the vote of the people, his body was dumped into the river. If he was decidedly good, his body was taken and placed in his tomb.

The Sioux Indians of the Dakotas claimed to have visions of death. They claimed they could see a particular person dying in their dreams. If death occurred at home, the family would wait for one day and one night hoping the person might revive and live again. As soon as they were sure of death, the women would cry aloud. They cried loudly enough to be heard throughout the camp.

Proper procedure demanded that all of the relatives dress the body in its finest attire. Eagle feathers were placed in the hair and various masks were painted on the body of the deceased. Next to the body were placed those items most cherished in his lifetime. The body was then wrapped in a robe, and a tanned skin was folded and placed on the chest. The body was tied up to resemble a bundle. Next, a scaffold was built on four high posts. After this, the adult members of the family would undergo a worship ceremony. Men ran pegs through their arms and legs, women slashed their limbs or cut off their fingers at the first joint, and both men and women cut their hair short. All of this was voluntarily done to indicate grief and sorrow. Men and women would weep and wail for four days as they marched around the camp and under the scaffold. After four days, the body was removed from the tepee and tied to the scaffold. This process in itself was a procession. All of the individual's belongings were attached to a pole at the head of the scaffold. Additionally, his horse was killed and the tail was placed on the pole.

On the first day of air burial, the tribe would wail, eat, and smoke pipes in an effort to relieve all passions they had held for the deceased. Over the next three days, they would remain sober and quiet. They would leave their homes only to hunt and fish. Furthermore, they would not sleep during these days. After the four days were up, they would continue to mourn for four months and present gifts to the dead. The corpse, after these four days of rites, was buried in a shallow grave on a hilltop or in a special place. A simple stone was placed at the head of the grave and a fence was built around the grave to keep animals and spirits away. The stone contained information regarding the dead Indian's life, people he had killed in battle, and any other information believed to be important.

Children were protected from the spirits of the dead by tying roots from trees around their wrists. This protected them against the devil or various spirits in which the tribe believed. Additionally, children were not allowed to linger around or see the body of the dead.

The Salish Indians of the Northwest United States would leave a dying person in the woods near their village. They would send an old man with him and the dying person would confess all of his misdeeds. Not doing this would welcome a ghost who would haunt him after death. Just before death, the dying person was placed in a high tree so that animals could not get near him. If he died during the night, he would be buried the next afternoon. Before burial, volunteers would prepare the body. As it was not considered an honor to do this, it was often difficult to find volunteers. The dead were buried in shallow graves in rocky cliffs. Like the Sioux procedure, a fence was put around the grave to keep animals away. Speeches, prayers, singing, and eating were all customary at the funeral of a Salish Indian.

After the funeral, the dead's belongings were given to those people within the tribe who needed them most, and the house of the dead was burned. It was forbidden for the mourning wife to remarry for two to three years, and she was not permitted to sing or work during this time span. Furthermore, mourners were required to wear their oldest clothing as an indication of grief.

The Navaho Indians of the Southwest United States had still different death customs. A singer was brought in to sing for the dead person. The dead were buried as quickly as possible with their possessions including their saddle, blanket, and tools. They were laid in caves with ashes placed in front of them to ward off ghosts. Post-burial activities were similar to those of the Salish Indians.

Eskimo death and burial customs are to some extent dependent upon the environment in which they live. Since the ground is frozen solid in the Eskimos' environment, except during the summer months (when it thaws to a depth of one or two feet), few Eskimos bury their dead underground. Cremation is not used either because it is considered a wasteful process in an area where fuel is scarce. Some of the methods used by the Eskimos in disposal of the dead are surface burial, casting the corpse into the sea, and placing the body on sea ice where it will eventually sink. Additionally, Eskimos of the Bering Sea place the dead in wooden boxes that are secured in position above the ground by stakes.

Various types of graves in which the body is protected by stones are used extensively. The most highly developed form of the stone grave takes the shape of a rectangular structure covered with large flat stones, over which smaller ones are piled.

Another common method of disposal of the dead is out-and-out exposure. Some Eskimos simply lash the limbs of the deceased to the body and expose the corpse to the elements, removing it from the sight of the community or camp. When a body is exposed, it naturally becomes prey to animals, most likely the dogs belonging to the people themselves.

There are local customs that govern the orientation of the body in the grave with reference to geographical direction, sometimes depending on the age and sex of the person. The Eskimos either lay their dead in a flexed or extended posture. The flexed burial is probably most common. This doubled-up position has the advantage of reducing the size of the grave. Furthermore, it is a common practice to bind or lash the dead body. It is generally believed that doing so restricts the departure of the ghost from the body. However, among Eskimos who do not fear the ghost, bindings are cut when the body is fully deposited in the grave.

In Eskimo procedure, the dead are shown respect by having their implements and weapons placed with them in the grave. Gifts such as furs and utensils are often made to the family of the deceased in great quantities. In the case of an expected death, such gifts are collected for years in advance. After the mourning period has passed, all those involved take a sweat bath (a type of sauna). This bath serves as a final cleansing ceremony and allows the Eskimo mourner to resume the normal affairs of life.

A rigid system of taboos and requirements control the Eskimo during the period of mourning. It is not uncommon for the bereavement period to last from four or five days to a year. To show love for her husband, the wife of the deceased does not wash for a whole year after the death. Nor does she look toward the sky or over the sea, speak above a whisper, or eat certain foods.

Another typical custom is a taboo of working with sharp instruments such as needles, picks, or knives. This is to prevent accidental injury to the ghost, which is thought to be present following his death. Mourning taboos on hunting and eating also exist. When a person dies, his soul is believed to retain the need for bodily nourishment. Therefore, offerings of food are made at the grave or at a festival for the dead. Also, mourners will not eat anything for a set period of time hoping that this self-denial will please the spirit of the dead person. There are also restrictions on hunting during the mourning period. The major reason behind most of these mourning customs is to attempt to forestall the evil powers of the ghost.

Some of the mourning and burial customs and procedures of the ancient Egyptians, Sioux and Salish Indians, and the Eskimos can be identified in today's funerary procedures. The more common concerns of respect for the dead and mourning are obvious.

Today, within the customs of the Catholic Church, the Sacrament of Annointing is given to the aged and terminally ill. In cases of sudden death, the same sacrament is given, but the prayers are geared to the suddenness. Viewings for the dead may be held in a funeral home, a person's home, or in the church. Regardless, it is usually arranged through the pastor of the church by the family of the deceased. At the viewing, a rosary or wake service is held. Many consider the viewing to be for the family as it supplies them with the satisfaction of seeing the person for the last time.

On the day of burial, the coffin is blessed with Holy Water at the entrance to the cemetery, thus indicating the sacredness of the body. The coffin is then covered with a Funeral Pall or white cloth. At the gravesite, a final farewell from the church is verbalized. The whole cemetery is previously blessed because of the sacredness of the bodies to be buried there. Any Catholic or nonCatholic member of a Catholic family may be buried in a Catholic cemetery.

When death occurs within the Amish community, friends and neighbors play an important role in the ensuing rituals. They make important decisions concerning burial procedures as well as making the very clothes that the deceased will wear.

Among the Old Order Amish, the body is prepared by the family. It is washed, but not embalmed. To conform to state laws, it must usually be buried within forty-eight hours. Under the newer, Progressive Order, the body is embalmed by a mortician who dresses it only in underwear and white socks. The body is then taken to the family home for proper dressing.

Coffins used by the Amish are of the older, European style. It is an elongated, hexagonal style that opens to reveal only the head and chest. Neither the interior nor the exterior contains any extravagant ornamentation. The interior is lined with plain white cloth and a white pillow, while the exterior is stained dark brown and has no handles.

Deceased Amish are dressed entirely in white. Women are dressed in a white dress and cape while men are dressed in a white shirt, vest, and broadfalls. The casket is placed on two sawhorses for the viewing of the body. No flowers or decorations are in or around the coffin.

The service is about two to three hours long and is usually conducted by at least four ministers. It is held either in the barn or the house of the family and consists of a sermon, scripture readings, and an eulogy. No music is played before, during, or after the service. Almost all ages attend the service. Hence, eight hundred people is not an unusual number to find at an Amish funeral.

While the service is going on, *hoslers* (young boys) take care of the buggies and horses that are used in the procession. The procession leaves the home en route to the cemetery that, for the Old Order, is usually located in an open field, and for the Progressive Order, is usually behind the church. A service is held at the gravesite where the casket is opened for a final viewing. The grave is hand dug by friends and does not include a vault (a cement casing into which the coffin fits). The coffin is lowered by means of leather straps in front of the viewers as part of the graveside service. The headstone is oblong with a rounded top and bears only the deceased's name, dates of birth and death, and parents' names.

After the service, the friends and relatives return home for a meal prepared by friends. Memorial poems that resemble ballads are made up to tell of the events leading to the death of the deceased. They are printed in *Budget*, an Amish newspaper, and given to the closest surviving relatives who usually put them in a family notebook or Bible. They are said to aid the family in the mourning process.

All in all, you can see that Amish customs are basic and simple, heavily relying on friends for comfort at the time of death. Since they accept the will of God, fear of death is not common. The Amish believe that friends will meet again in the life of the world to come.

The service for Moslems varies slightly in different countries. The general procedure, however, is as follows.

Moslems usually say, "It is the will of Allah," to the deceased person's family. This fatalism is said to bring comfort in sorrow and to lessen the resentment. Within Moslem belief, it is not proper to keep the corpse in the house very long. As such, they usually bury it the same day or the day after death. For strict Moslems, funeral homes are not involved in the process.

In some segments of Islamic culture, when someone dies, all of the curtains are immediately taken off the windows as a sign of mourning. During the time before burial, mourners wail and scream for the deceased to show their grief. It is customary for the relatives to remain awake until the deceased is buried. Members of the family may wash the body or they may hire male and female washers to wash and shroud the corpse. Since there is no embalming, the body is kept on ice to slow the degeneration process.

During the viewing and the procession which follows a coffin may be used. But this is not always the case. When carrying the coffin or the corpse in the procession, no one is permitted to precede the corpse, for it is believed that angels walk before it. The service is not in the cemetery; rather, it is held in an open spot near the graveyard or in the home of the deceased. No singing or music is permitted before or during the service. At the cemetery, the coffin or the shrouded body is lowered into the ground in front of the relatives. If a coffin is used, the lid is left off, for it is the belief of the Moslems that if the lid is closed, the person's soul will not be able to rise. The corpse, coffin or not, is placed on its back in the grave with the head of the deceased to the north, the feet to the south, and the face turned east toward Mecca, the birthplace of Mohammed and spiritual center of Islam. With these words, "We commit thee to earth in the name of God and the religion of the Prophet," the body is placed in the ground.

On the third day following burial, relatives visit the grave to say more prayers. No bright colors are worn during this period of mourning, and soiled clothes remain unchanged. Then, on the fortieth day after the death, all of the relatives visit the grave and later have a celebration. The spirit of the deceased is said to roam for forty days, and it is on this fortieth day that the spirit finally finds peace and joy in Heaven (or pain in Hell).

The Hindus of India place great importance on the preparation of the body for burial and on additional ceremonies. Following death, the Hindu's body is laid out with flowers draped over him and a lamp placed at his head. The navel is smeared with oil, cotton is placed in the nostrils, the big toes are tied together, the eyelids are closed, and the hands are folded across the chest. While Hindus traditionally consider the funeral a celebration, women must mourn. If a male has died, women must continue to follow certain steps. These steps include various anointing rituals. Mortuary specialists conduct the rituals of burial and the burial itself.

Following the anointing rituals, a frame is constructed on which the body is laid. Various decorations of religious significance are placed on the framework or *bier*. A procession is formed at the house of the dead Hindu. The procession is usually led by the eldest son or the nearest relative while the widow always remains at home. Cremation is most often used as a means of body disposition. After body disposition, many of those who die in India are brought to the Ganges as it is considered a sacred river. It is by Benares, the holy city, and is fronted with concrete and marble slabs upon which heaps of combustible materials are laid (*pyres*). The procession reaches the pyres and the body is removed from the bier. It is then immersed in the holy water and placed on the pyre as a brief disposal ceremony is given. The person who led the procession lights the pyre. Prayers are recited by attending priests as the body burns. The procession continues to march around the pyre but no one is permitted to look directly into the fire. After the cremation, the mourners take a purification bath in the holy river and make offerings to ancestral spirits.

Three days following the cremation, relatives gather at the pyre and collect bones. The bones are thrown into the river to assure the release of the soul from the deceased. Further rituals continue for ten days to ensure the soul of acquiring a new, complete body.

When a death occurs in China, one of the older relatives must rush to the nearest temple to inform the local god of the death. The family of the dead hangs blue and white or blue and yellow lanterns from the door to inform others in the community that a death has occurred. Meanwhile, the family weeps in the room where the death has occurred. Following this, the body is bathed and wrapped in wadding (cotton in specially prepared sheets) and clothed. The feet are tied together as a precautionary measure to keep the body from jumping about due to evil spirits. The body is laid out on a bed while the coffin is prepared. The coffin, large and bulky (weighing as much as three hundred fifty pounds), is constructed in such a way that it tends to preserve the body for extended periods of time. As the body is laid in the coffin, various kinds of clothing are packed around the body.

During this time, the family prepares the house for a reception. Some of the items used in the preparation are vases with paper flowers, candlesticks, incense sticks, and an oil lamp. All of these are placed symbolically on a table at the head of the coffin. Additionally, a spirit tablet that has the name of the deceased printed on it is placed on the table. Various religious authorities are summoned to the home to carry out religious ceremonies. Sons, daughters, nephews, nieces, even grandchildren attend the mourning ceremonies. Guests generally bring gifts to the ceremony that often seem to make it more like a celebration. However, signs of happiness are nonexistent. Male and female mourners are expected to wear specific types of clothing. Hair styling and other outward appearances are designed to demonstrate mourning.

The funeral procession is a glorious occasion involving many individuals and using symbols to glorify the dead. The burial and last rites do not complete the mourning period. Three days after the burial, mourners return to give food and burn money for the spirit. Additional ceremonies occur on the twenty-first, thirty-fifth, forty-ninth, and sixtieth days after the death. Mourning behavior of the family continues for one year after the death of their beloved. Additionally, the Chinese people have festivals in the spring, summer, and autumn designed to honor the dead.

Jewish death customs dictate that those present as the death takes place recite "Blessed be the true judge" in Yiddish. A glass of water and a strip of linen may be placed by the bedside immediately following death so that the soul may bathe and dry itself. In medieval times, the body was prepared by the Hebrah Kaddisha, a burial organization. The preparation, known as the Tahara, began with the cleansing of the body from head to foot, using tepid water. The fingernails and toenails were cut, and the hair, after being cut, was neatly combed. The body was then dressed in burial clothes. However, the role of the Hebrah Kaddisha has been taken over by commercial undertakers.

Today, the rabbi gives a eulogy at the funeral chapel. A funeral oration is not given over the body of one who has committed suicide. The ceremony is often spoken in Yiddish, which is the vernacular of the Jewish faith. It is customary for the members of an organization to which a dead male belonged to conduct the entire service. However, the rabbi or chaplain may assist. Following the recitation, there is a procession to the cemetery. The Kaddish, the mourner's prayer, is recited just before the grave is filled.

The body is usually buried within one or two days following death. This time period may be expanded if the family wants to wait for relatives living at a distance. Prior to burial, the hands of the dead are either bent to form the outline of the word *Shaddai*, (Almighty), or wooden forks are placed in the hands to enable the deceased to burrow his way to Palestine on the day of resurrection. The use of coffins is now universal among Jews, although orthodox and conservative still use plain, undecorated ones.

Following the completion of the service and recitation of the Kaddish at the gravesite, all those who have participated in the funeral wash their hands either at the chapel or the house of mourners. A "meal of condolence" follows the service and consists of a large variety of simple and easily prepared foods. Orthodox and conservative Jews observe seven full days of mourning. Many American Jews observe only three days. During this time, friends of the deceased visit the mourners at their home. They often bring with them meals of condolence.

At the end of one full year after the death, a monument or tombstone is erected in memory of the deceased. This unveiling, at the gravesite, usually takes place on a Sunday so that all who wish to attend may. It is conducted by a Rabbi who reads a regular service. Furthermore, twice each year, a candle is burned in remembrance of the deceased. It is lit at sundown and left to burn. These two days serve as anniversaries of the death.

Death and burial customs and practices take different forms depending on the actual customs and beliefs of a particular society. However, some basic elements and procedures remain similar.

Burial procedures are often identified as activities that visually confront the mourners and reaffirm the reality of the death. This visual confrontation marks the beginning of the healing process. This support, which manifests itself in the social and psychological dimension, is an important function of the funeral. Furthermore, most death and burial procedures are religiously oriented indicating an overall cultural belief in some type of life after death.

Almost all burial procedures include a procession of some sort that begins at the place of the funeral and ends at the place of disposition. This final step, disposition of the dead body, takes place in one of four ways:

1. Earth, or burial under the ground
2. Cremation, or burning of the body
3. Water, or disposing of the body to the sea
4. Air, or exposure to the elements for natural degeneration

Preparation of the Body for Burial in the United States

Tread lightly, she is near
   Under the snow,
Speak gently, she can hear
   The daisies grow.

All her bright golden hair
   Tarnished with rust,
She that was young and fair
   Fallen to dust.

Lily-like, white as snow,
   She hardly knew
She was a woman, so
   Sweetly she grew.

Coffin board, heavy stone,
   Lie on her breast,
I vex my heart alone,
   She is at rest.

Peace, peace, she cannot hear
   Lyre or sonnet,
All my life's buried here,
   Heap earth upon it.

(OSCAR WILDE   "Requiescat")

We have already looked at some of the world's religions and how they prepare the body for burial. Let us now turn our attention to that preparation most often used in the United States: the process of embalming.

Embalming, now a professional science in the United States, can easily be dated back to ancient Egypt. Egyptian mummies were preserved by means of bitumen (a combination of various hydrocarbons such as asphalt, tar, and petroleum), spices, and/or natron (a mineral). In fact, as early as the twelfth century, a physician known as El-Magar prescribed bitumen that was drained from the skulls and stomachs of mummies for sick patients. He had maintained that this substance aided in the healing of bruises and wounds. As recently as three or four hundred years ago, drained bitumen formed one of the ordinary drugs in the pharmacist's shop in England and Ireland. After a while, the supply ran short and 'treated' bitumen had to be manufactured. Physicians would take the bodies of dead criminals and have them filled with bitumen. The bodies would be exposed to the heat of the sun for a period of time and the 'treated' bitumen would be drained and used as before.

The Egyptians had different processes of embalming that ranged in expense. In the most expensive method, the brain of the dead was drained through the nose with the use of an iron hook, and then the cavity was rinsed out with various drugs. Next, an incision was made in the left side of the abdomen with a sharp stone. The abdomen was drained and rinsed out with palm wine and then sprinkled with a perfume. The body was filled with spices and perfume, sewn up, and left to soak in bitumen for seventy days. After this time span, the body was wrapped in bandages made of flaxen cloth that were smeared with gum. Finally, the body was coffined and set upright against the wall of a temple.

In what can be termed a "middle expensive method," the abdomen was injected with oil and placed in a bath of natron for seventy days to prevent the oil from flowing back out of the body. After seventy days, the oil was allowed to flow from the body bringing with it the internal organs. This left only the skin and bones, which were then wrapped in flaxen cloth and set in an upright coffin in a temple.

In the least expensive method, the abdomen was rinsed with syremea, (a preservative chemical), and left to soak in a bath of natron for seventy days, after which it was removed and wrapped in a flaxen cloth and put in a coffin.

Additionally, the length of the embalming, traditionally seventy days, was dependent upon the type of ceremony. As a profession, embalming was passed down from father to son. Embalmers in Egypt were greatly respected. Prices and standards were set in writing. Decisions regarding the type of method and cost that could be afforded were dependent upon the relatives of the dead man.

The question of 'why' Egyptians embalmed their dead is indeed an interesting one. Budge claims that the first Egyptians made no attempt to mummify their dead, mainly because they did not possess the necessary knowledge. With the development of funeral ceremonies and procedures for mourning their dead, the Egyptians seem to have acquired the techniques for embalmment. It has been suggested that embalming rituals endowed the dead body with the power to withstand decomposition, thus assuring it everlasting life with the gods. Furthermore, the soul was believed to be distinct from the body. However, the survival of the soul was dependent upon the survival of the body. Hence, preservation of the physical body meant preservation of the soul. Van Daniken, among others, suggests that archaeological finds support the belief that prehistoric humans believed in a physical return for a second or more lives. Surely embalmment can be seen as an approach to immortality. Whether the type of immortality desired was spiritual or physical in nature is still questionable.

Embalming today is not a universal practice. In fact, it is not a process inherent to civilization as many of us think it is. In England, for example, embalming is not legally required. In fact, only a minority of the English do embalm. Basically, there is a small demand for such a process. This is not the case in the United States. While embalming laws vary from state to state, it is not generally necessary, nor legally required, to embalm the dead except in special cases. It is recommended, however, that if the body will not reach its destination within twenty-four hours, it should be embalmed. The smell and sight of deterioration begins within this time span. Hence, all bodies prepared for viewing should be embalmed, whereas if the body is to be buried within twenty-four hours, such a process is not absolutely necessary. Contrasting this, almost all states require either embalmment or an airtight sealed casket for bodies infected with dangerous communicable diseases, or those that will be shipped by common carrier.

Likewise, most state laws require embalmers and/or funeral directors to have a minimal education and apprenticeship prior to opening up a practice. A typical educational program includes two years of college (sixty semester credits) at an accredited college, one year of mortuary school, and one year of apprenticeship during which time the apprentice must help prepare approximately twenty-five bodies. Additionally, he must successfully conduct a funeral, making all of the arrangements. Mortuary school includes courses in embalming, restorative art, funeral directing, mortuary law, accounting, public speaking, bacteriology, pathology, and chemistry.

Let us now turn our attention to the most common step-by-step approach of the preparation of a body for burial in the United States.

Step I: Removal

After a funeral home has been called, the body will be moved to the funeral home. The funeral home will most likely have to go to the home of the deceased, the hospital, nursing home, or possibly to the scene of an accident.

Step II: Family Visit–Legal Aspects

Second, the funeral home will set up a time for the family to discuss their wishes for the handling of the dead. Such necessary issues include the type of casket desired, type of vault, if desired (legally required in some areas), clothes for the deceased, (sold by the funeral home or supplied by the family), and total costs. Additionally, a number of forms must be completed. Typically, these forms include:

1. Death Certificate: This is necessary for stocks, bonds, title changes, banking and checking accounts, insurance policies, and property ownership.
2. Application for burial expenses for a deceased service person (if applicable): At the present time, a deceased veteran is entitled to up to four hundred dollars from the federal government and one hundred dollars from service fraternities such as Eagles, Moose, or Elks. All of these funds can help meet funeral expenses.
3. Application for burial expenses for a deceased serviceman's widow (if applicable)
4. Application for burial benefits: This allows two hundred-fifty dollars for burial and funeral expenses, and one hundred-fifty dollars for interment and a burial plot allowance.
5. Application for the United States Flag for burial purposes (if applicable): The flag is laid over the casket during the funeral and given to the family afterwards.
6. Application for headstone or marker: Anyone who fought in wars for the United States is entitled to this.
7. Statement of death by Funeral Director
8. Funeral Purchase Record

Step III: Setting Features

Prior to embalming, the body is given a complete bath. The mouth is given a realistic appearance and the deceased's own dentures are used if possible. Cotton is used to fill out the cheeks or simulate teeth, however, wax may be used and molded into a natural shape. The mouth is closed permanently. It may be stapled or sewn shut. The deceased is given a shave and haircut if necessary. Finally, plastic caps are inserted onto the eyeballs. These are like contact lenses, and they are structured to hold the eyelids closed. If the eyes are donated, the sockets are filled with cotton.

Step IV: Embalming

Embalming begins with an incision, used for drainage, in one of three places. The femoral artery and vein in the leg may be used, however, there is usually much fatty tissue in this area which makes the use of these difficult. The axillary artery and vein in the arm may also be used, though this is usually awkward. Most preferred are the carotid artery and the jugular vein, which are located in the neck. These are the largest, and hence, the easiest to use.

The incision, a two inch cut, is made so an aneuryem hook can be inserted to pull the carotid artery and jugular vein to the surface. An arterial tube is placed in the carotid artery pointing down toward the feet. The arterial tube is hooked up to an embalming machine which contains the proper mixture including embalming fluid. This machine can regulate both the pressure and rate of flow. A drain tube is placed in the jugular vein and is also pointed downward toward the feet. This tube is hooked up to a sink for drainage. The embalming machine is then turned on and embalming fluid is pumped into the body. All blood is forced through the jugular vein and out of the body. This process may be repeated two or three times to be sure that all of the vessels are flushed out. Fluid passes to the head cavity by means of what is termed "bypass circulation." This process does not have to be repeated for the head. An efficient and experienced embalmer can tell by sight and feel when the body is fully embalmed.

Next, a trocar (a long vacuum tube with a sharp point) is inserted through the abdominal wall and into the bottom of the stomach, heart, lungs, liver, bladder, and other organs. The trocar is moved around at random to pick up all blood, fecal matter, urine, etc. The direction of flow is then reversed and embalming fluid is pumped into the cavity.

Step V: Dress

The funeral director then proceeds to dress the deceased as though he were still living.

Step VI: Casket Placement

The body is removed from the embalming table and taken to a casket that was previously selected by the family. This is done by hand or by various lifting devices for heavier deceased persons.

Step VII: Cosmetic Preparation

A final step in this process includes the use of makeup in the funeral parlor itself. Lights that will be on during the viewing are turned on. During this step, the funeral director may use various creams, skin dyes, etc., for basic color and highlighting effects. A funeral director may use the deceased's own cosmetics for a more natural look.

At this point, the body is said to be prepared for viewing and burial. The embalming procedure has disinfected the corpse as well as retarded natural decomposition.

Special cases exist where a body has been mutilated in an accident. These cases call for different procedures with the end result being the same; disinfection and retardation of decomposition. Occasionally, a body will be so badly mutilated that embalming is next to impossible. These cases usually result in closed casket viewings.

In short, the duties of a funeral director, other than preservation of the deceased, include legal guidance and completion of all necessary forms, an obituary notice sent to a local newspaper with relevant information decided upon by the family, consultation with the clergyman, consultation with cemetery personnel, formulation of memorial folders presented at the viewing, consultation with the doctor, providing help in the selection of clothes and a casket, arrangement of flowers and recording their origin, and serving as a host at the viewing.

Cremation

There are strange things done in the midnight sun
  By the men who moil for gold;
The Arctic trails have their secret tales
  That would make your blood run cold;
The Northern Lights have seen queer sights,
  But the queerest they ever did see
Was that night on the marge of Lake Lebarge
I cremated Sam McGee.

(ROBERT W. SERVICE   "THE CREMATION OF SAM McGEE")

Cremation is the process whereby the body is reduced to ashes by means of fire and heat. There is enough archeological evidence to suggest that cremation was widely practiced among prehistoric cultures. The origin of cremation can be dated back to the Stone Age when it was used in eastern Europe and the Near East. Excavations have uncovered urn fields (burial grounds) in sections of Europe believed to have been deposited between 1500 and 800 B.C. The remains (ashes and charred bones) were found in urns of various designs. Uncremated remains were also found in the same general area implying that both cremation and earth burial were practical forms of body disposition during that time period.

There is also evidence to suggest that cremation was generally practiced among ancient Greeks and Romans. It is hypothesized that cremation, as a form of disposition, was practiced by ancient Greeks around 1000 B.C. Some archeologists suggest that it was used for the purpose of sanitation. Others suggest it was used for religious purposes because cremation was denied to those who committed suicide, infants, lightening victims, and any others who might not be favored by the gods. Furthermore, it was typically an upper-class phenomenon as it was quite expensive.

Romans probably acquired the practice from the Greeks. Early cremation occurred in Rome as early as the sixth century, B.C. As was the case in Greece, it was an upper-class practice. Poorer people could not afford the expensive fuels for incineration.

Historically, cremation was not practiced (and was actually resisted), by ancient Jews and Christians for religious reasons. The Jews believed that only criminals and animals should be treated in such a way. Christians resisted cremation for various reasons. Primarily, they felt, like the Jews, that cremation was an inhuman act showing little or no respect for the body of the dead. Secondly, they feared that cremation might interfere with resurrection.

Like the ancient Greeks and Romans, many ancient Asian cultures practiced cremation. Among them were the cultures of Japan, Tibet, Thailand, and India. The Shinto religion (the native religion of Japan) allowed cremation even though it was not used with any regularity. Zen and Tendai Buddhists in Japan permit either traditional burial or cremation. Cremation in Tibet was typically used only where fuel was plentiful. Interestingly, the ashes of cremated Tibetans were cast into medallions that were placed in special places to serve as memorials.

In Thailand, it was a tradition that the body be embalmed and preserved for a specific time period dependent on social status. After this time factor was satisfied, one could be cremated. Cremation in India may have begun as early as 2000 B.C. Because of religious and philosophical influences, cremation was believed to break the body into its basic elements: fire, water, earth, and air. It was believed that by doing this the spirit was purified and prepared for reincarnation. Great care was taken regarding performance of the ritual and, depending upon the sect, the ashes were either scattered or buried.

In summary, primitive cremation was based on spiritual beliefs, for example, to ward off evil spirits, to facilitate the soul's ascent with the upward movement of the flames, or to expedite reincarnation. Roman authorities often cremated bodies of Christian martyrs for different reasons. They believed that this prevented the Christian's soul from rising from the dead. After this, the Judeo-Christian culture labeled cremation as paganism. Since Western culture modeled itself after the Judeo-Christian example, cremation has been used only in emergencies such as plague, natural disaster, or gross battlefield casualties.

Primitive North American Indians practiced cremation on special classes of individuals. The primitive Miami Indians cremated those who they believed to be victims of witchcraft while the primitive Choctaw Indians cremated those who died away from home so they could transport the ashes back to their home for burial. Other primitive Indian tribes burned only the bodies of warriors slain in battle, while still others limited cremation to the diseased.

For many centuries cremation was looked down upon by religious and legal authorities. Then, around the latter part of the 19th century, cremation was reinstated into Western culture. This interest affected Italy, Germany, England, and the United States at about the same time. Italy moved toward the idea of cremation for health reasons in 1872. Legalizing the process followed the development of an improved furnace that accomplished cremation efficiently and inexpensively while minimizing pollution to the atmosphere. However, it was not until 1876 that the practice was actually instituted in the northern portions of Italy. Germany, approaching the issue at approximately the same time as Italy, established the first German crematorium in Gotha, Germany in 1878. Both social and religious approval was slow to follow.

Modern day cremation is said to have actually begun with the forming of the Cremation Society of England in 1874 by Sir Henry Thompson. His initiative and support was a direct result of his dissatisfaction with English graveyards. He was not alone in his fear regarding the possibility of the spread of disease. Others who supported cremation at this time included Anthony Trollope, Spencer Wells, Millian, the Dukes of Bedford and Westminister, and George Bernard Shaw.

In the United States, the topic was first discussed at occasional assemblages in New York around 1873. The first crematory in the United States was constructed in 1876 by a prominent physician for use by his friends. Then in 1881, both the New York Cremation Society and the United States Cremation Company were organized. They built and operated a crematorium in 1884 in Lancaster, Pennsylvania. By 1900, there were about twenty-four crematories operating in fifteen different states in the United States.

Recent studies have shown that cremation has become increasingly popular in densely populated countries. The International Cremation Federation indicates that seventy-five percent of the Japanese, fifty-seven percent of the English, and smaller but similar percentages of the Swedish, Danish, Swiss, and Czechoslavakian people utilize cremation in dealing with disposal of the dead. In fact, cremation is now permitted either by law or custom by three-quarters of the world's inhabitants. [However, only about five percent of the deceased in the United States are cremated each year.] Most of the cremations performed in the United States are in heavily populated cities and tend to be an upper-class phenomena. Additionally, religious attitudes play a role in acceptance of cremation. (These attitudes will be mentioned in a following chapter.)

The process of cremation in the United States is rather simplistic in nature. However, since there are virtually no remains, determination of the cause of death is impossible after cremation. Hence, some legal forms must be completed before cremation is allowed. This is to prevent destruction of the evidence of any possible crime or wrongdoing that may have been committed to the corpse. The body must be free of suspicion of murder. If one were murdered and cremated shortly thereafter, all evidence of such a crime would be destroyed.

The process involving the funeral service and cremation can occur in one of four ways in the United States. In the first way, the body is prepared for viewing. Afterwards, the viewing and funeral service take place as usual. Finally, the body is taken to a crematorium rather than a cemetery. Mourners often go to the crematorium at this time. They may view the actual cremation although this is not usually suggested. In the second method, the funeral service is held at the crematorium chapel and cremation follows. A third option is to have the body prepared, then taken to the crematorium for the viewing and funeral. The final option is to have the body taken directly to the crematorium following death. In this instance, the body is cremated first and a memorial service can be held whenever the family wishes. Hence, funeral services may be held at a crematorium chapel, at the deceased's place of worship, or at a funeral home. The service may be held prior to cremation, later over the remains, or both. In all but the fourth option, ceremonies involving committal of the body are preestablished by the crematoriums and may vary from one crematorium to the next.

The body and the casket are then placed in a special furnace called a retort. This furnace is entirely enclosed except for vents through which the gases escape. The body and the casket are then subjected to intense heat. The gases are recirculated through open heat chambers so there is very little discharge into the open air. The retort may be heated by gas, oil, or electricity. Most undertakers insist on a casket. This seems to be an unnecessary added expense. Some undertakers suggest that a casket creates a "memory picture" of the deceased and serves a bereavement function. However, there is no evidence of a state law requiring a body to be in a casket for cremation in any of the United States. In earlier days, the body was removed from the casket and only the body was cremated. Now, according to the "Manual of Standard Crematory-Columborium Practices" published by the Cremation Association of America, a 'suitable container' must be utilized in the cremation process. This can vary from cheap wooden caskets to elaborate, expensive wooden or metal caskets. It is left up to the discretion of the crematory management as to what is 'suitable' and what is not. The process itself takes less than two hours. The body and the casket are reduced to anywhere from six to twelve pounds for adults. Metal fragments from the wooden casket are removed by magnet. If a metal casket is used, the remains are collected from within the remaining structure. The remains, commonly referred to as ashes, are then placed in an urn. The bones are pulverized by a machine and added to the ashes in the urn. The urn may have an identification of the deceased that corresponds to an epitaph on a cemetery grave marker.

There are several options available for the disposal of the ashes. The urn may be placed in a columborium (a dedicated enclosed place often maintained at a cemetery) or in a mausoleum. The stone or metal urn, if taken to a columborium, is perpetually cared for. It is available for viewing in its own little niche. This method, termed inurnment, is the most common in the United States.

The urn can also be buried in an earth grave. This method is most often used by those who have already purchased a cemetery plot. Small plots, usually owned by the crematory, may also be purchased for urn burial. These types of urn burials usually take place a few days after the cremation.

A third alternative is to have the ashes in the urn scattered over land or water. The English have been doing this for years. They have a special garden called the "Garden of Remembrance." This ground is consecrated, i.e., it is declared sacred for just this purpose. Some western states still have laws against scattering ashes over the ground or waters, but California legalized the scattering of ashes in 1965. The law at that time required that the ashes be scattered from at least five thousand feet above the ground or from three or more miles out at sea. (This law has been liberalized as we shall see later in this chapter.)

A fourth alternative is for the family to keep the ashes in an urn.

They may dispose of them in their own way, whenever or wherever they desire. Regardless of how the ashes are disposed of, the Cremation Association of America ". . .strongly recommends that such a service be conducted to dignify the disposition of the ashes as something more than mere discard."[1]

The "facts" surrounding crematory management and regulation demonstrate an unworkable relationship between crematories and funeral homes. Of the more than two hundred crematories in the United States, only a small number are owned and operated by funeral homes. The majority are owned and operated by cemetery managers. For those owned and operated by cemetery managers, a conflict of interest does not exist. For those owned and operated by funeral homes, that conflict does exist. Various state laws require the participation of licensed funeral directors for either burial or cremation. Hence, cremation management is dependent upon funeral directors for legal purposes. Funeral directors fear advocates of cremation for various reasons. They identify cremation advocates as people who wish to change the funeral practices and procedures that have been established by tradition. In short, a funeral director will be reluctant to mention the possibility of cremation unless it is one of his direct services. It can further be suggested that fear of economic loss by funeral directors has much to do with their perspective.

Some of the positive aspects of cremation deal with sanitation and hygiene, economics, and land preservation. Embalming, in a typical funeral/burial procedure deals with sanitation and hygiene. Those to be cremated must also be embalmed if there is to be viewing prior to the cremation. Economically, cremations are less expensive than regular funeral/burial procedures. In 1974, the average cost in Chicago, Illinois was one hundred dollars (for just cremation). If one wishes to store the ashes in an urn for shipping, burial, or placement in a niche, the cost may vary from fifty-five dollars for a simple urn to over five hundred dollars for a more elaborate one. However, the major cost is the purchase of space in the columborium which may range from fifty to seven hundred-fifty dollars, depending on the size, location, and quality of the niche.

Preservation of land is indeed a realistic rationale supportive of cremation. If one looks at all of the land devoted to cemeteries and considers the additional land that will be necessary in the near future to bury our 208-plus million population, the square footage of land required seems mind boggling. If the standard grave were to take up an area of approximately eighteen square feet of surface earth (which would be a rather conservative estimate), the 208 million people presently in the United States, would take up 3,744,000,000 square feet for burial when they die. This translates into about 85,950 acres. Washington D.C. takes up about 44,160 acres of space. The amount of land necessary to bury our present population would be twice the amount that is offered by Washington D.C. While we will obviously not bury all 208 million in Washington D.C., that bit of statistical calisthenics was merely to indicate that while this generation of people cannot foresee a problem, the problem does exist for future generations. It is our responsibility to solve the problems of tomorrow by offering solutions today.

Burial at Sea

Prayer unsaid, and mass unsung,
Deadman's dirge must still be rung:
  Dingle-dong, the dead-bells sound!
  Mermen chant his dirge around!

Wash him bloodless, smoothe him fair,
Stretch his limbs, and sleek his hair:
  Dingle-dong, the dead-bells go!
  Mermen swing them to and fro!

In the wormless sands shall he
Feast for no foul gluttons be:
  Dingle-dong, the dead-bells chime
  Mermen keep the tone and time!

We must with a tombstone brave
Shut the shark out from his grave:
  Dingle-dong, the dead-bells toll!
  Mermen dirgers ring his knoll!

Such a slab will we lay o'er him
All the dead shall rise before him!
  Dingle-dong, the dead-bells boom;
  Mermen lay him in his tomb!

(GEORGE DARLEY "The Sea Ritual")

In the past, there were many reasons for sea burial. Three basic reasons were:

1. The body was diseased, thus carrying the threat of disease to all crew members.
2. The voyages were long and there was no means of storing the body.

Hence, decomposition would begin and carry the odor of decomposition throughout the ship.

3. There were many superstitions, among which carrying a dead body was considered to be one of the worst.

Traditionally, death at sea was a solemn event. The dead were treated with respect and dignity. In the past, because of long voyages, losing a crew member was like losing one of the family. Additionally, once the sea burial was complete, someone else would have to assume the missing person's station or job.

According to past naval customs, the process of sea burial had six basic steps:

1. Upon death, the body was taken to the sailmaker.
2. The man on duty at the helm was informed of the death. He in turn would notify the captain.
3. The sailmaker would wrap the body in a canvas sheet. He would place a heavy object in the sheet near the feet. The canvas was stitched up with the last stitch going through the sailor's nose.
4. When the body was ready, it was carried out onto the deck for the dead sailor's final night watch.
5. The next morning a call was made, "All hands to bury the dead." The procession would come out with all ranks reversed to show the equality of death.
6. After the captain said a prayer, the body was dumped into the sea.

Today, burial at sea is somewhat different. It tends to follow a custom set forth by former seamen. The seaman would ask to be cremated and have his ashes sprinkled at sea. Although there are many variations, a typical sea burial today might be something like this. After death, the body is cremated and the remains are placed in an urn. The urn is taken out to sea by ship. The ship is then pointed into the wind and the ship's flag is lowered to half-mast as the engines are turned off. The captain recites a prayer and/or whatever else is desired by the family of the deceased. As the last words are said, the ashes are sprinkled into the sea.

Why would anyone desire this process? The answer is understandably simple. A traditional burial requires the purchase of scarce and costly land space, as well as the costs inherent in embalming, a casket, and viewing. Interestingly, both burial and cremation involve the natural process of oxidation that returns the body to its natural elements. However, cremation does this more rapidly and less expensively.

The prospect of sea burial is so appealing that two organizations have been formed in California for just that purpose. One of them, the Telophase Society, was founded in 1971. Telophase was the first organization to completely bypass the conventional cemetery/mortuary system. Upon notification of death, the body is transported to a repository at Telophase where it is held until a legal death certificate is obtained. Telophase then procures a cremation permit and takes the body to the crematory. Final disposition of the ashes is dependent upon the member's previous instructions. There is neither embalming nor viewing. Memorial services can be arranged for any time or any place since the dead body is not present.

Telophase approaches the concept of death from a very realistic view. They refer to the body as merely a 'shell of bone and tissue' that confines the real person . . . the self . . . life. As logic follows, why should so much be spent on preparation and care of the shell when it is the other aspects with which we are so concerned throughout life? The organizers of Telophase pride themselves in not taking advantage of the vulnerability of the mourner due to initial grief reactions. They maintain that they do not try to 'sell' anything to the survivors. Everything is prearranged at a present cost of two hundred-fifty dollars for members and three hundred dollars for nonmembers. This includes cremation, memorial services, and disposition of the ashes.

As of this writing, Telophase Society has approximately nine thousand members. In December of 1975, Telophase cremated over one hundred bodies. Over ninety percent of these were taken to sea. In California, the first legal statute for sea burial was passed in 1965. (This was indicated earlier in this chapter.) It made the cremation-sea burial process very expensive because it required that only one cremated body at a time could be taken out to sea in an airplane. Additionally, the airplane was required to fly at an altitude of five thousand feet and proceed beyond the three mile limit before the ashes could be dispersed. Recently, an amendment has liberalized that law. Now, any number of body remains can be transported at one time. Furthermore, the transporter, which may be either boat or plane, is not restricted to traveling beyond the three mile limit. In fact, ashes can be dispersed off the end of a pier as long as the container is retained. A cardboard type container can be utilized for this purpose; however, it cannot be used for shipping, burial, or for placement in a niche.

It is interesting to note a conflict of interests between Telophase and the funeral home-cemetery complex. The former is reportedly under pressure from monopolistic funeral organizations. The following indicates an example of this:

1. California statutes define the 'sea' as an 'interment' if ashes are deposited there.

2. To offer 'interments' a 'cemetery broker's license' is required.
3. To obtain a 'cemetery broker's license', one must be a full-time salesman under a 'broker' for two years.
4. Two such 'brokers' compete in San Diego. However, neither of these brokers wish to render services to Telophase, i.e.; they do not wish to hire a salesman from Telophase so that he can obtain a 'cemetery broker's license'.

Obviously, both brokers fear boycott by conventional cemeteries. Brokers get most of their business from cemeteries. Telophase, on the other hand, offers an alternative to cemeteries.

A second organization promoting the use of sea burial as an alternative to the mortuary-funeral-cemetery system is called The Neptune Society. Founded in 1973 by Dr. Charles H. Denning, Jr., the organization has grown to its present size of seven offices throughout California. Claiming over fifteen thousand members, The Neptune Society is devoted to a complete cremation service. Much like Telophase, The Neptune Society is on call twenty-four hours a day. Upon notification of death, the body is removed and taken to a repository where it remains until a death certificate is signed by the appropriate legal officials. Legal documents necessary for cremation and disposition are taken care of by the society. After cremation, the body is disposed of according to the deceased's wishes. However, the deceased must be a member of the society. (The cost for nonmembers is significantly higher). Membership fees are fifteen dollars for an individual and twenty-five dollars for couples. Present rates for cremation and dissemination of the cremated remains is two hundred fifty-five dollars. The Neptune Society claims that this is about one-eighth the cost of a conventional funeral. Additionally, The Neptune Society indicates that most people in California who desire cremation (about twenty-five percent in Southern California) also wish to have their ashes scattered at sea.

Both the Telophase Society and The Neptune Society offer an inexpensive, yet dignified alternative to the more traditional and costly system that may involve embalming, cosmetology, a casket, limousines, a grave, a tombstone, and other extra expenses.

SUMMARY

The attitudes and beliefs of past, as well as present, religious and cultural groups influence their preburial and burial procedures. As such, the Egyptians, Sioux and Salish Indians, and the Eskimos all showed great respect for the dead as their funeral procedures were designed to enable the dead to proceed to a life beyond their worldly existence. Furthermore, their funerary procedures visually confronted the mourners with the dead, thus confirming the reality of death.

The belief in some form of life after physical death was present (and still is) across most cultures. This is shown by the religious orientation of most preburial and burial activities.

Ancient Egyptians were the first recorded culture to embalm their dead. Now, in the United States, embalming is a professional science. It is not, however, a universal procedure. In the United States, embalming is only one of six steps that funeral homes go through in preparation of the body for burial.

Cremation, as a method of disposal of the dead body, was practiced by early cultures. Some cultures preferred cremation to burial largely for religious reasons. Realistically, cremation simply speeds up the natural process of decomposition. Today, cremation is much less expensive than a more traditional burial.

Burial at sea was necessary in the past to avoid the problems associated with decomposition of the dead body on long journeys. Today, sea burial usually follows cremation and the ashes are sprinkled into the ocean.

──────────────── **NOTES** ────────────────

1. Paul F. Irion, "Cremation Today," *The Individual, Society, and Death,* ed. by David W. Berg and George C. Daugherty, (Berg and Daugherty, 1972), p. 82.

──────────── **SELECTED BIBLIOGRAPHY** ────────────

BERKET-SMITH, KAJ, *Eskimos.* New York: Crown Publishers, Inc., 1971.

BERNARD, HUGH Y., *The Law of Death and Disposal of the Dead,* pp. 21–26. Dobbs Ferry, New York: Oceana Publishers, Inc., 1966.

BUDGE, E. A. WALLIS, *The Book of the Dead.* New York: University Books, Inc., 1960.

BUDGE, E. A. WALLIS, *The Mummy: Egyptian Funeral Archaeology.* London: Cambridge University Press, 1893.

BUDGE, E. A. WALLIS, *Sociology of Death,* ed. by Glenn M. Vernon, p. 218. New York: The Ronald Press Company, 1970.

GARDET, LOUIS, *Mohammedism.* New York: Hawthorn Books, 1961.

GROLLMAN, EARL A., *Concerning Death: A Practical Guide for the Living.* Boston: Beacon Press, 1974.

HABENSTEIN, ROBERT W. AND WILLIAM M. LAMERS, *Funeral Customs The World Over.* Milwaukee: Fulfin Printers, Inc., 1960.

HASSRICK, ROYAL B., *The Sioux.* Norman, Oklahoma: University of Oklahoma Press, 1964.

HENDIN, DAVID, *Death As A Fact Of Life,* pp. 151–60. New York: Warner Paperback Library, 1974.

HOSTETLER, JOHN A., *Amish Society.* Baltimore, Maryland: John Hopkins Press, 1968.

IRION, PAUL, *Cremation.* Philadelphia, Pennsylvania: Fortress Press, 1968.

IRION, PAUL, "Cremation Today," *The Individual, Society, and Death,* ed. by David W. Berg and George C. Daugherty, pp. 80, 82, 87. Berg and Daugherty, 1972.

LANTIS, MARGARET, "Alaskan Eskimo Ceremonialism," Monograph of the American Ethnological Society, pp. 9–20. New York: J.J. Augustin, 1947.

LOVETTE, LELAND P., *Naval Customs, Traditions, and Usage.* Annapolis, Maryland: U.S. Naval Institute, 1939.

MITFORD, JESSICA, *The American Way of Death.* New York: Simon and Schuster, Inc., 1963.

MURPHY, ROBERT CUSHMAN, *Logbook For Grace.* New York: The MacMillan Co., 1947.

NATIONAL FUNERAL DIRECTORS ASSOCIATION, "What Do You Really Know About Funeral Costs?" p. 5. United States, September 1974.

SHAY, FRANK, *A Sailor's Treasury.* New York: W.W. Norton and Co. Inc., 1951.

STRUB, G. AND CLARENCE L. G. FREDERICK, *The Principles of Embalming.* Dallas, Texas: Lawrence G. Frederick, 1959.

TELOPHASE SOCIETY OF AMERICA, "Complete Cremation Services." California: 1975.

VALENTINE, VICTOR P. AND FRANK G. VALLEE, *Eskimo of the Canadian Arctic.* Toronto: McClelland and Steward Limited, 1968.

VERNON, GLENN M., *Sociology of Death*, pp. 212–43. New York: The Ronald Press Company, 1970.

VON DANIKEN, ERICH, *Chariots Of The Gods?* p. 80. New York: Bantam Books, 1972.

WEYER, EDWARD MOFFAT, *The Eskimos*, pp. 261–87. New Haven, Connecticut: Yale University Press, 1932.

7

Various Attitudes Toward Cremation and Medical Care

For everything there is a season, and a time for every
matter under the heaven,
a time to be born, and a time to die;
a time to plant, and a time to pluck up what is planted;
a time to kill, and a time to heal;
a time to break down, and a time to build up;
a time to weep, and a time to laugh;
a time to mourn, and a time to dance;
a time to cast away stones, and a time to gather stones together;
a time to embrace, and a time to refrain from embracing;
a time to seek, and a time to loss;
a time to keep, and a time to cast away;
a time to rend, and a time to sew;
a time to keep silence, and a time to speak;
a time to love, and a time to hate;
a time for war, and a time for peace.

(ECCLESIASTES 3:1–3)

Different religions hold different viewpoints on various aspects of death
and medical care. To examine these viewpoints seems a worthwhile
intellectual endeavor. The three aspects to which we will turn our attention are:

1. Disposal of the body (cremation)
2. Donation of body parts and/or body
3. Euthanasia

We have concerned ourselves with each of these as a topic, so they
should be familiar to you. The pages that follow summarize these concerns.[1]

Religion[a]	Cremation	Transplants and Donation of Body or Parts of the Body	Euthanasia[b]
Assemblies of God	Individual decision	Individual decision	Individual decision
Baptist	Individual decision	Individual decision	Individual decision
Buddhist Churches of America	Acceptable	Acceptable depending on situation	Acceptable depending on situation
Christian Church (Disciples of Christ)	Acceptable	Acceptable/ Encouraged for Donor	Individual decision
Christian and Missionary Alliance Church	Discouraged	Generally acceptable	Opposed
Christian Scientist	Acceptable	Individual decision (unlikely for C.S. to desire such)	Opposed, un- acceptable practice
Church of the Brethren	Acceptable	Acceptable	Individual decision
Church of Christ (Christian)	Acceptable	Individual decision	Unacceptable practice
Church of Jesus Christ of Latter-Day Saints (Mormon)	Discouraged	Individual decision	Forbidden
Church of the Nazarene	Permitted	Individual decision	Unacceptable practice
Episcopal Church	Permitted	No theological objection	Unacceptable practice
Evangelical Covenant Church of America	Individual decision	Individual decision	Individual decision
Greek Orthodox Church	Not condoned	All except donation of entire body is acceptable	Unacceptable practice
Hindu	Cremation is only one acceptable	Acceptable	Not practiced (Unacceptable)
Islamic Society	Unacceptable	Acceptable	Unacceptable practice
Jehovah's Witnesses	Individual decision	Forbidden	Unacceptable practice

Religion[a]	Cremation	Transplants and Donation of Body or Parts of the Body	Euthanasia[b]
Judaism	Not in keeping with Jewish law	Consultation with rabbi's: decision-making is complex	Unacceptable practice
American Lutheran Church	Acceptable	Encouraged	Unacceptable practice
Lutheran Church (Missouri Synod)	Individual decision	Individual decision	Opposed
Wisconsin Evangelical Lutheran Synod	Unacceptable	Acceptable (question still exists on heart transplants due to rejection factor)	Opposed
Mennonite Church	Individual decision	Acceptable	Acceptable with some qualification
Quaker Religious Society (Friends)	Individual decision	Individual decision	Acceptable
Reformed Church of America	Individual decision	Acceptable/ Encouraged	Unacceptable practice
Roman Catholic Church	Unacceptable	Acceptable with some qualifications	Acceptable
Salvation Army	Acceptable	Acceptable	Unacceptable practice
Seventh-Day Adventists	Individual decision	Acceptable	Follows the medical ethics of prolonging life
Unitarian Universalist	Preferred to burial	Acceptable	Acceptable
United Church of Christ: Congregational	Acceptable	Individual decision	Generally condemned
United Methodist Church	Acceptable	Acceptable/ Encouraged	Generally discouraged
United Presbyterian Church	Acceptable	Individual decision	Individual decision

[a]Where Churches have no stated official position on these topics, it is assumed that the decision is one of individual choice. Also, in the matter of cremation, even if a church forbids this practice as a matter of individual decision, most allow it in cases of sanitary regulations.

[b]For *Euthanasia*, individual decision usually implies a matter of concern between the patient, his family, and the doctor.

From the previous chart, we can calculate the percentage of religious orders that have pro or con beliefs regarding cremation, transplantation, and euthanasia.

For cremation, we find that about seventy percent of all these religions believe cremation is either acceptable or an individual choice. Twenty-three percent find cremation unacceptable; seven percent prefer it to burial.

As for donation of the body or body parts for transplantation, eighty percent find the practice totally acceptable. Seventeen percent find it acceptable with some exceptions, and only three percent find the practice unacceptable with reference to the church's teachings.

Church doctrines are changing slowly regarding euthanasia. Notice that we have not included mercy killing in this discussion; however, almost ninety-nine percent of the churches listed here oppose mercy killing. Sixty percent of the churches find euthanasia in direct conflict with their teachings. About thirty-three percent totally accept euthanasia, while seven percent accept it with some reservation.

Obviously, if you follow the teachings of your church, you should become aware of its position on each of these matters. Differences of opinion between you and your church's teachings should be discussed with church officials.

NOTES

1. This information is abstracted from *Religious Aspects of Medical Care* (St. Louis, Missouri: The Catholic Hospital Association, 1975).

8

Grief and Mourning

I tell you, hopeless grief is passionless;
   That only men incredulous of despair,
   Half-taught in anguish, through the midnight air
Beat upward to God's throne in loud access
Of shrieking and reproach. Full desertness,
   In souls as countries, lieth silent-bare
   Under the blanching, vertical eye-glare
Of the absolute Heavens. Deep-hearted man, express
Grief for the Dead in silence like to death–
   Most like a monumental statue set
In everlasting watch and moveless woe
Till itself crumble to the dust beneath.
   Touch it; the marble eyelids are not wet:
If it could weep, it could arise and go.

(ELIZABETH BARRETT BROWNING "Grief")

It must be clarified that theories and hypotheses reflected in this chapter are just that, theories and hypotheses. Grief and mourning are not specific illnesses. They rarely follow a predictable sequence. Yet, the commonality among the theories suggests that some aspects of this process are identifiable. To be able to understand and identify these aspects will surely help us to adapt to our own or other's bereavement behavior.

Recent statistics indicate that as many as seventy percent of the deaths in the United States occur outside of the home. Many die within the impersonal confines of a hospital or nursing home. Because of this, the healing process of those close to the deceased is negatively affected. Various thanatological authorities conclude that in the bereavement process, much of the effectiveness of this process depends upon the recognition of the reality of the death by the mourners. Much of this reality is lost when families cannot experience the death process simply because it occurs away from home. As a result, grief therapy has found its way into the problematic area of bereavement. While it is not necessary for everyone to undergo grief therapy, some people do need help. Let us examine grief and bereavement, normal adaptation, abnormal grief reactions, and finally, grief therapy.

The loss of someone close to you is the loss of an important part of your identity. As such, your ability to function as an individual is affected. Grief is an illness that represents a significant departure from the bereaved's usual state of feeling, thought, and behavior. More specifically, Tobach defines grief as "...an emotional process generated by the irreversible dissolution of a psycho-social bond of the most evolutionary type."[1] Simply stated, grief is an emotional reaction related to social processes (the end of a social relationship). The human species has great ability to store and integrate past experiences. While animals have the same ability, it is generally believed to be on a more primitive level. Hence, when death occurs the social relationship is thrown into turmoil. Past experiences are reflected upon, but they cannot reverse the process of death. Grief may be accompanied, in varying degrees, by such complaints as lack of physical strength, difficulty in sleeping, lack of desire to eat, overeating, a sense of unreality and subsequent detachment from others, an intense preoccupation with the image of the deceased, a tendency to respond with anger and irritability, a self-condemning attitude resulting from feelings of guilt over what they should have done but neglected to do, a search for something to do but a lack of initiative to do it, restlessness, sadness, crying, suicidal thoughts, hallucinations, even delusions. In general, bereavement is characterized as a state of total depression. Depression is not just a state of mind; rather, it is a general illness. The effects of generalized depression result from the interrelatedness of the physical, social, and mental-emotional dimensions. This "interrelatedness" factor implies that the physical dimension of the individual cannot be affected without also affecting the social and mental-emotional dimensions of the individual, or the social dimension cannot be affected without also affecting the physical and mental-emotional dimensions, etc. This is to say that the skin, muscular system, cardiorespiratory system, digestive system, genitourinary system, endocrine system, and the nervous system (physical aspects) are all affected by the emotional aspects of bereavement mentioned before. Likewise, "emotional aspects" of bereavement are directly affected by the "social" loss or disruption of the bereaved's social system, i.e., friendship with the deceased is lost. Additionally, depression (often characterized as an emotional difficulty) is suspect to being the cause of a great many physical ills, including obesity, rheumatoid arthritis, heart failure, even cancer. Holmes and Masuda completed an extensive study in 1972. Among their findings, they suggest that the more your life changes, the more you are forced to adapt. This, in turn, lowers your resistance and makes disease more probable. Of forty-three life situation changes that led to illness or disease, the most serious were death of a spouse, death of a close family member, and death of a close friend, respectively. Furthermore, social problems resulting from the above include higher divorce rates among couples who have lost children and higher incidence of suicide among those who have just lost someone "close." Hence, the interrelatedness of the three dimensions complicates the seemingly simple problem of helping the bereaved adapt to the new life situation in which he finds himself.

Bereaved individuals, in order to compensate or adjust to the death of a loved one, may utilize a number of defense mechanisms. Among them, and perhaps the most basic of these, is repression. The individual's mind subconsciously represses his feelings. However, repression does not always work for numerous reasons. When it fails, the individual must find other ways to adjust. Some of the typical feelings and reactions of the bereaved and their resultant adjustment mechanisms are:

1. The bereaved may feel hostility toward the dead that may manifest itself in guilt. He may cope with this guilt by blaming the death on various medical personnel or family members ('they did not do all they could'). This removes the basis for his guilt feelings from himself and projects it elsewhere.

2. A bereaved individual may feel the need to be wanted. As such, he may find a substitution for his lost loved one. Such a substitution may take the form of increased activity in business matters, desire for increased response from colleagues, or establishment of a relationship with another person similar to his past relationship.

3. The bereaved may desire to have someone plan his life-style. He may wish to participate in certain activities under the auspices that he is behaving in a way that will make someone else happy. This indicates that he is denying his need for gratification.

4. Finally, but not exhausting the list of typical feelings and reactions, the bereaved may avoid environmental situations that remind him of the lost object. This behavior helps the individual to deny the reality of the death.

Summarizing the various feelings and emotional states as reactions to the death of a loved one, the bereaved may exhibit "...yearning, anguish, sorrow, dejection, sadness, depression, fear, anxiety, nervousness, agitation, panic, anger, disappointment, guilt, shame, helplessness, hopelessness, despair, disbelief, denial, shock, numbness, relief, emptiness, and lack of feeling."[2] All of these reactions, attitudes, and emotions are not atypical. Furthermore, there is ample evidence to suggest that the mourning process, as a series of reactions, enables the mourner to repair the social disruption and reinforce emotional-social ties with other family members.

Funeral rites play an important role in the reparation of social disruption. While the main object of funeral rites is the deceased, the resulting benefits are for the living. Funeral rites are thus intended to help the members of a group or family to adapt. As such, funeral rituals help individuals to adjust both socially and emotionally to the death of a loved one. In doing so, they aid in the reintegration of the family members into society and, hence, aid the survival of that society. As a result, funerals are important to all living individuals who comprise a specific society for the benefit of that very society.

Funeral rituals also aid the individual by providing a controlled environment in which he can express his anger or hostility. This helps to reduce the mourner's feelings of guilt or anxiety. If this anger is not worked out during mourning, the individual may become introverted and hold all of his feelings within. Funeral rites allow for this mourning process to take place. In fact, there is some evidence to suggest that the cost of a funeral may have significant importance on the effectiveness of this process.

Furthermore, it is a belief of some experts that cremation, as an alternative to the more traditional funeral-mourning process, tends to offer little to the mourner who must work through his emotions. The dead body, it is suggested, makes the funeral service specific. Even though there is usually a memorial service for cremations, the ceremony lacks individual identity because it lacks the presence of the body. Thus, the bereaved fail to emotionally realize the death.

Now that you are aware of some of the normal reactions to the death of a loved one, it seems reasonable to examine unwanted behaviors. The following summarizes behaviors that, while they are not abnormal, should *not* be actively sought. They are summarized from the work of Edgar Jackson.[3]

1. You should not condemn yourself. Nothing you do can turn back the hands of time. To dwell on such thoughts only retards the process of bereavement.
2. You should avoid the use of mood modifiers as this also interferes with the normal process.
3. You should avoid feeling sorry for yourself. Self-pity only confuses your normal thought behavior.
4. You cannot run away (geographically or emotionally) from the realization that the death of a loved one has taken place. You must face and resolve the issue of death that is emotionally disturbing.
5. You cannot withdraw from society. It is often difficult to face those around you, especially if they remind you of the deceased. Religious and/or social groups can be of much benefit to you in this time of need.
6. You should not be too concerned with what others might say. Although they often mean well, they may say things that do not make you feel better. However difficult, you should try to understand that they are only trying to comfort you.
7. You should not try to resolve all the issues confronting you at once. Take them one at a time and progress slowly, realizing that you may be temporarily off balance.

These are the major "do nots" as suggested by Jackson. To keep them in mind may help you adapt to that threat posed by the death of a loved one.

Grieving over the death of a loved one is a natural reaction; however, there are definitely unhealthy concerns within the grieving process. Three distinct cases of atypical grief reactions exist and should be identified. While they are atypical, they are only unhealthy to the extent that the mourner does not realize their existence at the time of mourning.

The first such reaction is termed the *Morbid Grief Reaction Syndrome*. The mourner in this case may delay or postpone mourning for weeks, months, or even years after the death of a loved one. He may show very little concern or reaction to the death when it occurs. This may result from confrontation regarding important tasks at the time of death. In effect, he transfers his concern away from the death experience to those tasks confronting him at the time. Such tasks usually include occupational endeavors.

The second reaction is termed *Anticipatory Grief*. This type of reaction is classified as one of the many forms of separation reaction. It is most often identified in individuals who have not experienced the death of a loved one but have experienced a separation. As such, normal grief reactions as previously discussed in this chapter, appear in individuals who have not witnessed a death; rather, they are separated from their loved one by war or recurring illness. The cause of the separation offers the threat of eventual death to their loved one. The grief reactions that follow serve as an emotional safeguard system in case the loved one dies. However, this can retard or impair a relationship if, in fact, the loved one returns. If the loved one returns and the mourner has effectively separated himself emotionally, then reintegration back into the family or preestablished social/emotional relationships is difficult. The occurrence of divorce among wives and soldiers, in which the husband later returned home after his anticipated death, is not uncommon. An example of anticipatory grief appeared in a recent newspaper article entitled "Accepted MIA's death years ago, widow says." The article identifies Carol Buckley as saying she had known of her husband's death for eight years. While indicating that the news of her husband's death had not caused a strong emotional turmoil because she accepted that he was dead many years ago, her acceptance of this fact was despite any direct knowledge of her husband's death. It was not until December 5, 1975 that the South Chinese admitted to President Ford that Lieutenant Commander Buckley had been killed August 21, 1967.[4]

Anticipatory grief is also likely to occur in cases of recurring illness. Death is anticipated every time a terminally diseased person returns to the hospital. Along with the normal grief reactions, recurring illness presents special problems. Apart from there being no immediate shock phase once death does occur, the end may in fact be marked by a sense of relief. In our culture "relief" following death is inappropriate. Hence, feelings of guilt and confusion concerning our thoughts accompany us.

Concerns created by the Morbid Grief Reaction Syndrome and Anticipatory Grief can be alleviated by means of awareness. Both the family and the physician can help the bereaved pass through these atypical reactions by understanding the type of problem he is facing. Otherwise, reactions to the death of a loved one may take the form of suicidal thoughts, drug dependence or alcohol abuse, and/or chronic hypochondriasis (an over concern with the state of our health without evidence of disease).

A third type of reaction can be termed *Pathological Mourning*. The mourner may indulge in a form of grief whereby he preserves every object that can be related to the deceased much in the same manner as it was before the deceased died. In essence, one may build a shrine. An example of this type of mourning behavior is Queen Victoria's extreme behavior following the death of her husband in 1861. The story is recorded as follows: Her husband, Prince Albert, died in 1861. The Queen immediately went into seclusion. She slept by his nightshirt keeping a cast of his hand not far away. She would occasionally reach out to touch the hand. Furthermore, she photographed the Blue Room so it could be kept exactly the same way as it was before her husband died. Physically and emotionally, the Queen's health diminished. She built various memorials to her dead husband including a mausoleum, London's Albert Hall, and a number of statues. She required fresh clothes to be laid out every day and hot shaving water supplied every night for her dead husband, Albert.

Obviously, Queen Victoria's bereavement was atypical, but this 'shrine building' and death denying behavior is not limited to her era. Many of these atypical reactions may require outside counseling to aid the individual in adapting to the threat posed by his own inability to adjust accordingly. Such counseling might include what is identified as *Grief Therapy*.

Grief Therapy exists as a counseling method for those who must learn to cope with the death of a relative, friend, or even a patient. While it may take a variety of forms, grief therapy is often used to educate those in medicine and associated professions to deal with death more effectively. The contemporary physician is reluctant to comfort the dying patient since he himself may not have a secure philosophy of death and dying. Hence, doctors may stop visiting the incurably ill since they do not feel as though they can personally deal with death or the dying patient. Likewise, nurses may protect themselves from becoming too emotionally involved, and even clergymen may abandon the family as soon as the funeral is over for these same reasons. Grief therapists attempt to reinforce the individual's ability to cope with death. They want to indicate that mourning is a natural and healthy reaction to death. But, it can also become a lonely and lengthy illness in which the mourner is frozen into permanent grief. Grief therapy, furthermore, hopes to prevent the pathological implications of bereavement. Hence, a trained grief therapist can help those mourners whose grief has possibly extended into neurosis find the basis of their feelings and learn to accept them.

Researchers find that almost all mourners experience what is called "strange or bad thoughts." These are thoughts that we are ashamed to admit or express. For example, when parents first hear the diagnosis of their leukemia-stricken child, they may wish their child to die soon. They are horrified by such a thought and may actually lose self-esteem. A grief therapist would point out that they really do not want their child to die. They just do not want to see their son or daughter suffer. Additionally, mourners often tend to blame themselves for the death of a loved one. These "bad thoughts" are a natural part of the grieving process, although everyone thinks his unacceptable thoughts are the worst. Someone trained in grief counseling can help others cope with their inner feelings and come to accept the death of a relative or friend sooner and more realistically.

Among the methods used by professionals experienced in grief therapy is a technique called "regriefing therapy." This therapy was developed by Dr. Vamik Volkan, of the University of Virginia, to end pathological mourning. Regriefing takes the patient through the original grief process a second time, this time, assuring that he accepts the death emotionally as well as intellectually. This involves working with the mourner's "linking objects" (these may be photos, toys, or other objects that remind the bereaved of the deceased). The fixation that the mourner may have for these objects must be broken so that dammed-up emotions can be released.

Grief therapists stress that the ego strength of the mourner should be reinforced so that he can accept possible feelings of guilt. The most significant problem in mourning is not guilt or loss, it is the ignorance of the grief process. When one finds that guilt, strange thoughts, and regrets are "normal" within the context of the grieving process, he can then begin the emotional journey back to a normal life. But, of course, as therapist Phyllis Taylor has aptly stated, "You never recover totally from a loss. Especially when you lose a child. All you can hope for is to learn to accept it and get on with living more sensitive living."[5]

Most recently, various programs have surfaced to provide help during the bereavement process. One such program, under the guidance of Dr. Phyllis Silverman, is called the "Widow to Widow" or "Widow's Aid" Program. Women who have lost a loved one and have had the experience of bereavement visit newly bereaved women. While they are not "professional" in the sense that they are trained, they offer help, friendship, and occasional advice. Dr. Silverman meets with the staff regularly to discuss special cases or problems. All in all, the program attempts to help the newly bereaved through the bereavement process. Other programs such as Parents without Parents, THEO (in Pennsylvania), NAIM (in Chicago), and POST-CANA (in Washington, D.C.), have also started in the United States and elsewhere. They take advantage of widows, clergymen, physicians, nurses, or just interested people who wish to help.

As we have seen, grief therapy can be accomplished by anyone, including specially trained psychologists, social workers, paraprofessionals, or friends and relatives. No matter who the therapist is, the universal rule pursued is encouragement of expression of feelings of grief and recognition of what these feelings really are. We should become aware of what grief is, so that when we face it at some inevitable point in our lives, we will have the ability to realistically cope with death. Let us look more closely at the normal bereavement process.

Bereavement may take many forms and may occur in varying degrees as well as at different times for individuals faced with the death of a loved one. The death of a loved one affects not only the individual's concept of the world but his or her self-concept as well.

How long does one suffer after the death of a loved one? What are some of the reactions of a person in mourning following a death? Neither of these questions can be answered explicitly. Research in this area, however, indicates that there is a general process through which a mourner passes. It encompasses a rather slow recovery from the impact of a death experience. During this time span, the death becomes a reality and the life of the mourner, with some readjustments, continues.

Some investigators of this phenomenon have divided this mourning process into phases. Bowlby, one such investigator, has suggested three phases of mourning that are not only observable in humans of all ages but also appear to exist in a number of species of animals. The first stage (nonpathological) is one in which the mourner angrily craves recovering the lost person. In doing so, he often appeals for help. The second stage is characterized by personal apathy and disorganized behavior patterns. This "new personality" that develops allows the mourner to relate to new objects and new people. During the final stage, the mourner is once again able to find some satisfaction in living as he has accepted the death.

The passage of time apparently heals the wound of loss. Just how long this time span is appears to depend on the individual's ability to adapt to his surroundings of which the deceased was formally a part. The formation of new relationships within or outside of this environment also plays a role in this time period. Variables that are also involved in the length of mourning may include the age of the mourner, emotional closeness to the family of the deceased, the relationship with the deceased, and the mourner's overall attitude toward death.

Paul extends Bowlby's hypothetical three phases to include an underlying phenomenon that he terms pseudoreorganization, a false third stage. The third stage, as described by Bowlby, may be a mere imitation. The phenomenon of pseudoreorganization may hide the fact that the first two stages have not been completely worked out by the mourner.

From a recent study of death attitudes, another set of stages or phases through which a mourner passes following the death of a loved one may be hypothesized. Utilized in the study was an attitude scale designed to objectively measure attitudes toward death. The scale has met validity and reliability requirements.

The total questionnaire in this study included seven variables including Death Attitude Scale Score, age, sex, educational level (parent if unemployed), occupation (if unemployed, occupation of parent), religious beliefs, and recentness of death experience (How long has it been since an emotionally close friend or relative of yours has died?). This last question was responded to in numbers of months. It is with the first and last variables that this hypothesis was concerned.

The graph on page 135 contains plotted points of the mean death attitude score and the number of months since an emotionally close friend or relative has died. The mean death attitude score was computed for months in the following manner:

Death Attitudes for the First Thirteen Months

Letter A: Less than one month.

Letter B: One month or more, up to, but not including, two months.

Letter C: Two months or more, up to, but not including, three months.

Letter D: Three months or more, up to, but not including, four months.

Letter E: Four months or more, up to, but not including, five months.

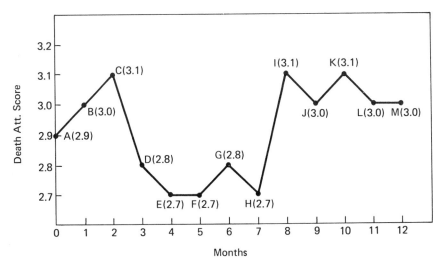

Letter F: Five months or more, up to, but not including, six months.

Letter G: Six months or more, up to, but not including, seven months.

Letter H: Seven months or more, up to, but not including, eight months.

Letter I: Eight months or more, up to, but not including, nine months.

Letter J: Nine months or more, up to, but not including, ten months.

Letter K: Ten months or more, up to, but not including, eleven months.

Letter L: Eleven months or more, up to, but not including, twelve months.

Letter M: Twelve months or more, up to, but not including, thirteen months.

As one goes through the mourning process, his or her attitude toward death changes. The data above graphically illustrates this point.

From the data provided, it is hypothesized that the mourning process can be identified as being comprised of five phases or stages that last about eight months before reorganization or acceptance of the death of a loved one can be identified.

Stage I: From time of death, up to, but not including, one month.
Shock/Denial

Kubler-Ross indicates that terminally ill patients pass through four stages prior to acceptance of their inevitable deaths. The first stage is that of shock or denial. He cannot believe that he is going to die. Likewise, the mourner's first reaction to the death of a loved one is shock or denial. He cannot believe a loved one has died. The mourner's reaction can be summarized as general numbness and disbelief. In short, he is attempting to deny that death has occurred. The mean death attitude score of 2.90 indicates an unacceptable attitude toward the death occurrence, i.e., an unwillingness to accept the death of a loved one.

Stage II: One month, up to, but not including, the second month.
False Acceptance
The mean death attitude score of 3.00 indicates an average attitude toward death. This can further be described as an apparent acceptance of the death. The mourner's attitude toward death is improved from stage one, but because of the stages that follow, this stage can best be described as "false acceptance."

Stage III: Two months, up to, but not including, the third month.
Pseudoreorganization
The mean death attitude score during this time span is at an all-time high of 3.10. This stage has been termed pseudoreorganization after Paul's work in this area. The mourner, in this stage, appears to have reorganized his or her life. It appears as though all systems are "back to normal." The data indicates that this stage of feeling is only temporary.

Stage IV: Three months, up to, but not including, eight months.
Depression
Approximately a five month stage of depression is indicated by unfavorable attitudes toward death: 2.80, 2.70, 2.80, and 2.70 respectively. Outwardly, everything may appear to be normal. We might even see this as an extension of Stage III. Inwardly, however, the bereaved person continues to question the loss of the loved one. The bereaved person may search his or her own memory for thoughts of the deceased. Although these thoughts tend to be happy remembrances, the underlying thought of the end of these 'happy experiences' with the deceased creates a negative or unfavorable attitude toward the death concept. Fluctuations in mean death attitude score appear during these five months. These fluctuations may identify fluctuations in the thought processes during the depression stage.

Stage V: Eight months and longer
Reorganization/Acceptance

Although the graph stops at twelve months, the leveling off as shown from month eight to month twelve continues into further months. Somewhere around the eighth month, the mourner finally accepts the death of a loved one. Mean attitude score, although fluctuating slightly from the eighth month on, levels off to a mean of 3.0. The mourner, in this stage, can see his loss in a new perspective. He is now able to clearly distinguish between the past and the present. The future also holds some promise for the mourner at this stage. He may feel a sense of weary relief at having worked through the grief process. However, he is now ready to approach the future and continue his life.

The overall implication of the data and subsequent discussion is that the mourning process extends itself for up to eight months. This process is normal and should be considered so by therapists, counselors, and close friends or relatives relating to the mourner. The feelings and emotions that the mourner felt and demonstrated were most likely normal. To understand these "fluctuating" stages of normal grief following the death of a loved one brings us closer to understanding the feelings of the mourner. It is not necessarily the time factor that is important, it is the fluctuation from shock, to false acceptance, to pseudoreorganization, to depression, and finally to reorganization that one should understand. The time factor merely allows us to examine each stage in its proper perspective. It allows us to understand so that we may be able to help others through this time period of mourning. More than this, however, it allows us to understand ourselves.

<hr>

SUMMARY

The majority of those who die today in the United States do so outside of their homes, usually in a hospital setting. This process usually deprives those who could learn much from the dying and death experience. Also of extreme importance is the deprivation of precious time with loved ones for those who are dying.

The loss of someone close to you is a loss affecting part of your social and mental-emotional identity. This process is usually described as grief. Grief is a generalized illness involving all dimensions of the human being. Furthermore, it is quite normal following a crisis situation such as death. Usually, we incorporate certain defense mechanisms to cope with death in our personal lives. This is also normal within certain boundaries. Therefore, funeral rites can be identified

as having an important role in the adjustment of the individual to a death.
Atypical grief reactions such as the morbid grief reaction syndrome,
anticipatory death, *and* pathological mourning *are not, in and by them-*
selves, unhealthy. They are only unhealthy depending on their severity. De-
pending on this severity, grief therapy may be necessary. Grief therapy is de-
signed to help the individual find the basis of his feelings. Hence, he learns to
accept his thoughts and feelings. Furthermore, "strange" or "bad" thoughts
during mourning are not abnormal.

Presently, a number of volunteer programs exist for those who need help
during the mourning process. The mourning process, like the dying process, can
be understood in terms of stages or phases. Hence, a series of stages through
which the mourner passes has been identified. Like Kubler-Ross' five stages
that terminally ill patients may pass through, the stages of mourning may not
necessarily occur in order. Some may recur or not occur at all depending upon
each individual's particular mourning process.

NOTES

1. Ethel Tobach, "Notes On The Comparative Psychology of Grief," *Loss*
and Grief: Psychological Management In Medical Practice, ed. by Bernard Schoenberg, Arthur C. Can, David Peretz, and Austin H. Kutscher (New York: Columbia University Press, 1970), p. 349.

2. David Peretz, "Development, Object, Relationships, and Loss," *Loss and*
Grief: Psychological Management In Medical Practice, ed. by Bernard Schoenberg,
Arthur C. Can, David Peretz, and Austin H. Kutscher (New York: Columbia
University Press, 1970), p. 13.

3. Edgar N. Jackson, "You and Your Grief," *The Individual, Society, and*
Death, ed. by David W. Berg and George G. Daugherty (George G. Daugherty
and David W. Berg, 1972), pp. 61–64.

4. "Accepted MIA's Death Years Ago, Widow Says," *Chicago Tribune,* December 7, 1975, Sec. 1, p. 5, col. 1.

5. Kron, Joan. "Learning To Live With Death," *Philadelphia Magazine,*
(April 1973) p. 85.

SELECTED BIBLIOGRAPHY

"Accepted MIA's Death Years Ago, Widow Says," *Chicago Tribune,* December 7, 1975, Sec. 1, p. 5, col. 1.

CATTELL, JAMES P., "Psychiatric Implications In Bereavement," *Death and Bereavement*, ed. by Austin H. Kutscher, pp. 153, 157. Springfield, Illinois: Charles C. Thomas, 1974.

HENDIN, DAVID, *Death As A Fact Of Life*, pp. 182–83. New York: W.W. Norton & Company, Inc., 1973.

HOLMES, THOMAS H. and R. H. RAHE, "The Social Readjustment Rating Scale," *Journal of Psychosomatic Research*, 11 (1967) 213.

HORN, JACK, "Regriefing: A Way To End Pathological Mourning," *Psychology Today*, 7, no. 12 (May 1974), 104.

JACKSON, EDGAR N., "You and Your Grief," *The Individual, Society, and Death*, ed. by David W. Berg and George G. Daugherty, pp. 61–64. George G. Daugherty and David W. Berg, 1972.

KNIGHT, JAMES A. and FREDERIC HECTER, "Anticipatory Grief," *Death and Bereavement*, ed. by Austin H. Kutscher, p. 197. Springfield, Illinois: Charles C. Thomas, 1974.

KRON, JOAN, "Learning To Live With Death," *Philadelphia Magazine*, (April 1973) pp. 85, 140.

KUBLER-ROSS, ELISABETH, *On Death and Dying*, p. 38. New York: MacMillan Publishing Co., Inc., 1974.

MEHRHOF, AUSTIN, "Jackson's Nine Areas of Concern," *Death and Bereavement*, ed. by Austin H. Kutscher, p. 166. Springfield, Illinois: Charles C. Thomas, 1974.

MENDELBAUM, DAVID G., "Social Uses of Funeral Rites," *The Meaning of Death*, ed. by Herman Feifel, pp. 189–217. New York: McGraw-Hill Book Company, 1965.

MITFORD, JESSICA, *The American Way of Death*. New York: Simon and Schuster, Inc., 1963.

NICHOLS, ROY AND JANE NICHOLS, "Funerals: A Time For Grief and Growth," *Death: The Final Stage of Growth*, ed. by Elisabeth Kubler-Ross, pp. 87–96. New Jersey: Prentice-Hall, Inc., 1975.

PAUL, NORMAN L. "Psychiatry: Its Role In The Resolution of Grief," *Death and Bereavement*, ed. by Austin H. Kutscher, p. 181. Springfield, Illinois: Charles C. Thomas, 1974.

PERETZ, DAVID, "Development, Object, Relationships, and Loss," *Loss and Grief: Psychological Management In Medical Practice*, ed. by Bernard Schoenberg, Arthur C. Can, David Peretz, and Austin H. Kutscher, pp. 11–13. New York: Columbia University Press, 1970.

PERETZ, DAVID, "Reaction To Loss," *Loss and Grief: Psychological Management In Practice,* ed. by Bernard Schoenberg, Arthur C. Can, David Peretz, and Austin H. Kutscher, p. 20. New York: Columbia University Press, 1970.

"The Psychology of Death," *Newsweek,* 76, no. 11 (September 14, 1970), 103.

ROSELL, ALAN, "Lindemann's Pioneer Studies Of Reactions To Grief," *Death and Bereavement,* ed. by Austin H. Kutscher, p. 163. Springfield, Illinois: Charles C. Thomas, 1974.

"Therapeutic Friendship," *Time,* 97, no. 18 (May 3, 1971), 45.

TOBACH, ETHEL, "Notes On The Comparative Psychology of Grief," *Loss and Grief: Psychological Management In Medical Practice,* ed. by Bernard Schoenberg, Arthur C. Can, David Peretz, and Austin H. Kutscher, p. 349. New York: Columbia University Press, 1970.

VERNON, GLENN M., *Sociology of Death,* pp. 157–65, 175. New York: The Ronald Press Co., 1970.

YORBURG, BETTY, "Acceptance of the Idea of Mortality," *Intellect,* 103, no. 2362 (January 1975), 215–16.

9

Funerals: Service or Rip-Off?

When I am dead, my dearest,
  Sing no sad songs for me;
Plant thou no roses at my head,
  Nor shady cypress-tree:
Be the green grass above me
  With showers and dewdrops wet;
And if thou wilt, remember,
  And if thou wilt, forget.

I shall not see the shadows,
  I shall not feel the rain;
I shall not hear the nightingale
  Sing on, as if in pain:
And dreaming through the twilight
  That doth not rise nor set,
Haply I may remember,
  And haply may forget.

(CHRISTINA GEORGINA ROSSETTI "Song")

Whether the services proposed by funeral homes in the United States are a necessity or a rip-off is a concern under attack in today's society. Jessica Mitford's, *The American Way of Death*, was one of the first public attacks on undertakers in this country. Hers was one perspective. Now that you are somewhat familiar with the services offered and provided by funeral homes, you may be better able to draw your own conclusions.

Of principal concern is the 'cost' factor. The three main costs are the casket, the vault, and the opening and closing of the grave. Embalming, an additional cost, is sometimes added into the price of a casket. As mentioned before, if one disregards the viewing, there is no legal reason for embalming, assuming that the deceased did not die of a communicable disease. A funeral director supplies itemized costs if one so desires. These costs, like other costs, depend to a large extent on the geographical location of the funeral home (New York City V. Small Town, U.S.A.). Considering the amount of work that a funeral home must do during the embalming process, the cost is understandably necessary.

The funeral home spends a minimum of ten person hours just preparing the body for viewing, and spends a total of sixty person hours per deceased for the entire funeral process. Since a director has what amounts to four years of college and is considered a professional in his area, multiply the number of hours times a paraprofessional or professional standard wage in your area. The cost of the casket, often including the entire cost of the funeral, also varies from area to area. A casket,

142

considered one of the main costs, is made of either wood or metal. Let us look at some of the elements of wood and metal caskets to further our understanding of this 'expense'.

Wood caskets are made of walnut, mahogany, cherry, maple, oak, hardwood, or tulip trees. No two wooden caskets are ever alike in appearance; the grains and pigments of each are different. Furthermore, most wood caskets are more expensive than metal caskets. Wood caskets proceed through at least eleven steps at the factory before you see the finished product.

Metal caskets are made of copper and steel and come in various colors such as blue, green, white, brown, and gold. The shapes of the caskets are all similar with only the handles and the ornaments making them look different. Metal caskets, easier to construct, pass through only eight steps before being delivered to the funeral home.

Each casket undergoes quality manufacturing with systematic inspections. Casket manufacturers are quite proud of their final products. Promotion and advertisements for caskets often include such terms as 'quality', 'elegance', 'distinction', 'beauty', 'uniqueness', and 'classic'. Casket companies, yielding to the average American's desires at a time of need, attempt to produce a product that is worthy of these terms.

The price of the total funeral process may vary from twelve hundred to more than two thousand dollars. Again, this depends on the area, but let us look at a small town cost analysis of an 'inexpensive' funeral.[1]

Itemized Expenses (As of January 1, 1976)

$125.00	Cost of casket (cloth covered)
35.00	Body removal from site of death (20 mile radius)
100.00	Embalming and preparation
150.00	Use of funeral home facilities
50.00	Professional services of the director
65.00	Use of hearse
50.00	Burial garments
25.00	Modest spray of carnations
10.00	Clergy honorariums
3.00	Death notice
200.00	Grave site
125.00	Opening and closing of grave
170.00	Vault (cement)
150.00	Grave marker (set-up included)
$1,258.00	Total cost

Comparing this to a large metropolitan area, let us look at a similar analysis of an inexpensive funeral in Chicago, Illinois. Since all figures are averages, it should be noted that prices may vary from one funeral home and cemetery to the next.

Itemized Expenses

$400.00	Cost of casket
45.00	Body removal from site of death
125.00	Embalming and preparation
240.00	Use of funeral home facilities
180.00	Professional services of the director
65.00	Use of hearse
30.00	Burial garments
10.00	Modest spray of carnations
25.00	Clergy honorariums
18.00	Death notice
275.00	Grave site
200.00	Opening and closing of grave
100.00	Vault (cement)
245.00	Grave marker (set-up included)
$1,958.00	Total cost

It is not difficult to identify those aspects in which the cost is considerably higher in a large metropolitan area. Interestingly, most Americans do not select the 'inexpensive' method. It has been stated that some people feel they should spend more in order to 'honor' their loved one.

Funerals in England appear to be less expensive. The cheapest funeral in England is sixty dollars, the "average" is one hundred forty dollars, and the most expensive is about two hundred eighty dollars. Why? First of all, undertakers or funeral directors are not required to be licensed. They are usually regarded as tradesmen. England has about one funeral director per eleven thousand people compared to one per seven thousand people in the United States. Funeral directors in England are not on twenty-four hour call as they are in the United States. In England, if one dies at any time other than during the working hours of the funeral director, the family will have to wait until the next day for removal of the body and subsequent preparation. Additionally, embalming is only required if the deceased has died of a communicable disease or must travel by air to the burial location. As mentioned before, only a minority of deceased people are embalmed in England.

In contrast to English simplicity, a recent newspaper article indicates the extent to which American casket companies will go to provide elaborate caskets. Jacwil Casket Company of Knightstown, Indiana now has a "patriotic" casket on the market. Red, white, and blue in color, it is adorned with two American flags. In the last eight months, about four hundred of these special caskets have been sold. The article title sums it all up, "Go Patriotic—Be buried in red, white and blue." In England, on the other hand, only ten percent choose caskets. The remaining ninety percent choose coffins that are basic kite-shaped boxes made of African hardwood or English elm. Also, burial vaults are rarely used. Viewings are held in a crematorium or a cemetery chapel with an average of six to ten people in attendance.

The above indicates only one possible explanation regarding the cost of a funeral; Englishmen do not go to the extremes that Americans do regarding funeral preparation and burial. Americans traditionally demand more; therefore, they must pay for more.

Before you form your decision as to whether funerals in the United States are a service or a rip-off, read the following interview and closing statements with a funeral director in a small town in the United States, (population approximately twenty thousand).[2]

QUESTION: How did you become interested in this profession?

ANSWER: I became interested in this profession when I was a young boy of about seventeen. I had always felt I wanted to be a funeral director. I lived near a very large funeral home in Philadelphia and was impressed with the type of people who worked there and was particularly interested in the work that they did. I think reading about the Egyptians and the skills required to preserve human remains prompted me to think more about becoming a funeral director. Therefore, it was because of the funeral home near my neighborhood and my interest in history and preservation of history that I chose my profession.

QUESTION: What schooling was required? For instance, what kind of courses did you have to take and where did you go to school?

ANSWER: I went to the University of Pennsylvania, the Wharton School. I went to Penn to get a full four year collegiate background. I felt that Penn would prepare me emotionally and mentally to cope with activities in the business world and would better prepare me to be a funeral director. Following my graduation from Penn, I went into industry and worked with the Bell Telephone Company of Pennsylvania for approximately ten years before I returned to the field that I felt I would like to spend the rest of my life in. However, the only schooling that is required is a minimum of two years at an accredited collegiate institution, followed by a twelve-month course at an approved school of mortuary science. There are about nineteen approved schools in the United States, the closest one in Pennsylvania being at the University of Pittsburgh. The schooling involves courses in embalming, restorative art, funeral directing, mortuary law, accounting, public speaking, bacteriology, pathology, and chemistry. These are the courses that I can remember offhand. There may have been some others, however, it is a full year of schooling and an interesting year at school. During that period of time, a student must prepare a minimum of seven remains for burial. Following the year at the approved mortuary school, a future mortician must serve a year-long apprenticeship with a licensed funeral director. He must be registered with the State Board of Funeral Directors and he or she must assist the funeral director in the conduct of his business throughout that year. The individual must prepare twenty-five bodies and have them certified as being prepared correctly by his preceptor. Then his activities are reviewed by the State Board of Funeral Directors at the completion of the year's apprenticeship. He must also, during that period of time, assist the funeral director and be given the opportunity to conduct a funeral, make arrangements for the funeral and, in general, complete all of the details that are involved in a funeral and again be critiqued and certified by the funeral director (preceptor) that he is working for. At the completion of that year, the applicant must sit for a written examination involving the various subjects he studied at mortuary school and then take a practical examination before licensed funeral directors indicating his ability to preserve human remains, demonstrate his skills along this line, and answer practical questions regarding the conduct of a funeral business. If he is successful in completing this examination, he is licensed in the state of Pennsylvania. Other licenses are available and an individual can obtain those licenses through the various state boards throughout the country. However, the licensing of a funeral director is completed by a state board of funeral directors who not only examine the qualifications of the individual funeral director but then, follow his licensure. Following the establishment of his own funeral business or practice in any community, they also follow up and inspect, from time to time, his facility and the conduct of his business.

QUESTION: What was your initial reaction to your first dead body? Do you think that as you progress in your profession you become less and less emotional?

ANSWER: I don't feel anyone can become less emotional in the funeral profession. The funeral business to me, as a representative of it, is a very emotional field. To me, it is not a business; rather it is a calling. My initial reaction to the first dead body I prepared was one of concern and mysticism. I was trying to understand specifically what was happening and what was going to happen. I might say I was a little bit queasy and squeamish about the whole affair. After the first preparation that I witnessed, I remember feeling emotionally drained. I don't really know how I could describe it in words. Adding to your question, I can't really tell you why I was emotionally drained as a result of my first experience in watching that preparation.

QUESTION: When you prepare a body, what do you think about? For instance, do you wonder what kind of person the deceased was, or what kind of a life he or she led?

ANSWER: Well, this is a difficult question. When I prepare a body, I generally know the individual that I am involved with, the particular client. I know him as a person, and in most cases, I know his family. I know things about his life, and in many cases, I've shared experiences with him. I am personally sad that he has lost his life because life is so wonderful, it's the most wonderful possession that any of us has. However, as I go about my particular task of preparing a body for burial, I think specifically of the honor he's brought me in considering that I should be the person to prepare his remains for burial. I also think in terms of trying to do the very best I can to restore his remains to as lifelike a condition as possible.

QUESTION: Do you react differently, emotionally, when preparing a child as opposed to an adult?

ANSWER: The preparation of any human remains is a sad emotional experience. As I indicated before, a life has been lost and life is precious, so for most funeral directors it is a sad experience. However, it is a necessary technique to follow and it is important to preserve the remains from a public health standpoint so that the health and safety of the community is preserved. When we're talking specifically of the preparation of adults, I think that most funeral directors would agree that when preparing an adult who has lived a long life (the Bible says three score year and ten is a long life, although today, in many cases, that is a short life), the feeling is generally that they've seen and enjoyed life. But what about a young child or baby? The thought is that they have missed this wonderful experience. Thoughts must go through the individual that is involved in the preparation as to why the child lost its life. There is sadness involved in that. Or, he thinks about what the child will miss in the form of experiences in life. And, finally, the relationship of that individual to its family, brothers and sisters, aunts and uncles, and parents becomes apparent. That's a very sad situation. All of these things are probably in the mind of the funeral director as he looks at a child whom he is preparing for burial. Most funeral directors would say that it is a very sad occasion.

QUESTION: Have you ever prepared one of your own relatives or someone very close to you? How would you, or did you, respond emotionally?

ANSWER: I would not prepare one of my own relatives or any immediate family member for burial. I couldn't handle it emotionally, nor do I feel that the majority of funeral directors could.

QUESTION: Do you ever become depressed being in this line of work?

ANSWER: No, not really. I feel that this profession offers a great opportunity to be of service to my fellow man as I assist them through one of the most difficult periods of their lives. This is the period when they have lost someone close to them, someone very dear, someone who in most cases has meant the difference between life and death to them, someone who in many cases cannot be replaced.

QUESTION: How do you cope with all the sadness and the grief? Do you emotionally disassociate yourself from the event, or do you think of death as something that you just can't fight?

ANSWER: Death is something that no one can fight. No one wins against this particular situation or fact of life. Death is final. How may one cope with sadness and grief? I think you can only adjust to sadness and grief. Most funeral directors are emotionally involved with their client and the emotional circumstances surrounding the death in that particular family.

QUESTION: How do you approach the dead person's family? Do you deal with them strictly in a business-like manner, or do you deal with them emotionally?

ANSWER: I approach every family very sympathetically. I do not approach them in a business-like manner. In most cases the families are close friends of mine and I can only approach them as such.

QUESTION: How do people react to you when you tell them you are an undertaker?

ANSWER: I think most people react to undertakers as though they are in a stereotyped group. Undertakers have been characterized over the years in many different ways, and perhaps in your own mind you have a stereotype of an undertaker. Although most people are curious, very few feel uncomfortable in the presence of an undertaker. They're generally interested in the funeral profession when they get to know the individual funeral director on a personal basis.

QUESTION: What kinds of personalities would you say undertakers have?

ANSWER: Most undertakers I've known have had pleasant, friendly personalities. I know of very few who have morbid personalities. I firmly believe that one would not be a successful funeral director very long if he had a strictly morbid personality.

QUESTION: Are you afraid to die? Do you accept death for yourself after having been around so many deaths?

ANSWER: No, I'm not afraid to die. Naturally I enjoy life, but I believe that in the Christian way there is a life after death. I

don't know exactly what that is, but I think it will be enjoy-
able and I hope I will be able to live a long life and then
enjoy a long death.

   In summary, the funeral director interviewed was very sincere
about his profession. He seemed both interested and concerned about
helping those people who came to him for his services. He regards
funeral directing as a calling rather than a business as exemplified by
relayed incidences where his services to the family continued for months
after the funeral was over. Also, he made it quite clear that for him, and
for many other funeral directors, this profession is a very emotional
field. It was pointed out that it is especially easy for one to become
emotional concerning this field in such a small town. As a result of his
geographical location, most of his clients are friends or acquaintances.
He emphasized that not all funeral directors react this way because there
are some who consider funeral directing strictly a business and nothing
else. Certainly there are those funeral directors who are out to make a
fast buck by attempting to sway customers toward expensive caskets
and funerals. As a consumer, we should spend the time and effort
necessary to locate a responsive director such as the one in our interview.

SUMMARY

*The costs of a complete funeral usually include the casket, the vault, the opening and
closing of the grave, embalming, and the additional services of the funeral
director. The caskets can be made of either wood or metal with wood caskets
generally being the most expensive. Casket makers pride themselves in the quality of their work.*

   *The total cost of a funeral is generally more expensive in metropolitan than
in rural areas. Funerals in other countries are less expensive than funerals in
this country. There are two basic reasons for this. First of all, funeral directors in
this country are professionals who attend four years of college. This is not true in
other countries. Secondly, Americans tend to demand more from funeral directors than do people in other countries.*

NOTES

1. Information in a letter to the author from Robert A. Allen, Lanterman Funeral Home, Inc., East Stroudsburg, Pennsylvania, January 21, 1976.
2. Interview with Richard J. Klofach, funeral director, Stroudsburg, Pa., by Jane Albright. Edited and reprinted with permission of Mr. Kolfach. January 21, 1976.

SELECTED BIBLIOGRAPHY

BERNARD, HUGH Y., *The Law Of Death and Disposal Of The Dead*. New York: Oceana Publishers, Inc., 1966.

FREDERICK, L. G. AND CLARANCE C. STRUB, *The Principles and Practice of Embalming*. Dallas: Lawrence G. Frederick, 1967.

HABENSTEIN, ROBERT W. AND WILLIAM M. LAMERS, *The History Of American Funeral Directing*. Milwaukee: Buflin Printers, 1962.

HUNT, GLADYS M., *Don't Be Afraid To Die*. Grand Rapids: Zondervan Publishing House, 1974.

NATIONAL FUNERAL DIRECTORS ASSOCIATION, *What Do You Really Know About Funeral Costs?* U.S.A., 1974.

STIFF, CARY, "Funerals: High Cost of Dying," *Chicago Today*, January 18, 1974, pp. 34, 47.

10

Longevity, Immortality, and Life After Death

Because I could not stop for Death,
He kindly stopped for me;
The carriage held but just ourselves
And Immortality.

We slowly drove, he knew no haste,
And I had put away
My labor, and my leisure too,
For his civility.

We passed the school where children played
At wrestling in a ring;
We passed the fields of grazing grain,
We passed the setting sun.

We paused before a house that seemed
A swelling of the ground
The roof was scarcely visible,
The cornice but a mound.

Since then 'tis centuries; but each
Feels shorter than the day
I first surmised the horses' heads
Were toward eternity.

(EMILY DICKINSON   "Time and Eternity: XXVII")

"Man is the only animal that contemplates his death; he is also the only animal that shows any sign of doubt of its finality."[1] To elaborate on this, man continues to think of the inevitable but refuses to believe it. He hopes for seemingly impossible extensions to his life. His goal is to exterminate death so that life may be endless, if not in its present form, then in another.

We have already discussed the possibility of extending life by treating death as the ultimate illness. Let us now turn our attention to a specific group or subculture of people where extended life is not an abnormality.

A Subculture Approaching Immortality!

Sula Benet, among others, has studied the Abkhasians of the village of Tamish in the Soviet Republic. Most of the one hundred thousand Abkhasians live and work on collective farms regardless of their ages. Interestingly, a good portion of this population ranges from age eighty to one hundred nineteen. The physical condition of this age group is remarkable. In an environment where the aging process seems to have ceased, the older Abkhasians work on a regular basis, many have their original teeth, and most have relatively good eyesight. They take daily walks with erect posture as though they were seventy years of age or younger. They take great pride in their physically healthy, slender bodies.

Benet visited the nearby village of Dzhgerda and reported seventy-one men and one hundred ten women between the ages of eighty-one and ninety. What is more, she found nineteen people over the age of ninety-one years. This translates into fifteen percent of the total village population of twelve hundred being over age eighty-one. The last year in which overall figures for the Abkhasian subculture were available was 1954. At that time, 2.58 percent of the Abkhasians were over age ninety. Comparing this rate to the entire Soviet Union and United States populations, .1 percent and .4 percent were respectively over age ninety. It does not take a mathematical background to realize that there *is* a difference.

To what do the Abkhasians attribute their longevity? There are a number of factors that enter the realm of rational explanations. Abkhasians place extreme importance on their diet, sex, and labor practices.

Diet was one of the variables most often researched. Basically, they have a stable diet, i.e., they eat the same foods throughout their lifetimes. Since overeating is considered an illness among these people, their diet does not significantly change even if their economic status improves. Although they consume twenty-three percent less calories than industrial workers of the same subculture, they take in nearly twice as much vitamin C. This is especially interesting in light of the current controversy regarding vitamin C. Dodi Schultz, among other experts in the field of nutrition, informs us that researchers do not yet know the long term effects of massive doses of vitamin C. In fact, there is some professional agreement that large amounts of vitamin C are indirectly responsible for kidney stone development in some individuals. If this is true, it certainly cannot be supported by reviewing the diets of the Abkhasians. Separate studies regarding these people have continued since 1932. Two separate researchers have found that arteriosclerosis, when present, was found only in extreme old age. Furthermore, the aged in this culture were extremely psychologically and neurologically stable. Note that this is what researchers *have* found. Of more importance is what they have not found. There is no indication in their findings of those typical physiological and psychological disorders that often accompany old age in other parts of the world. While there is mention of communicable diseases among the older individuals ("old" being around age ninety), there is little evidence of the presence of degenerative diseases such as cancer or heart disease. Perhaps much of this is due to their dietary habits. At any rate, they have increased their life span and hence, put off their appointment with death.

Abkhasians eat very slowly; therefore meals may last several hours. This is, of course, a direct contrast to the American attitude in which eating is simply a requirement for living that is carried out as quickly as possible. Americans want more time for other activities such as work or recreation. The actual eating procedure is also indicative of the Abkhasian attitude. They chew their food very slowly. Physiologically we know that this procedure allows for the flow of ptyalin and maltase, which in turn allows for the proper digestion of carbohydrates.

Abkhasians rarely eat meat but do include a daily intake of fresh fruits and vegetables, cheese, and buttermilk. Sugar is also excluded from their diet although honey is moderately used. They do not smoke cigarettes or drink alcohol to any great extent. (A locally produced dry red wine of low alcoholic content is present at most meals in small quantity.) Compare this to American dietary habits. Americans tend to eat quickly, chew quickly, include meat in at least two out of three meals, and take in large amounts of sugar.

Abkhasians also differ from Americans regarding other aspects of life. For example, sexual relations and marriage in Abkhasia tend not to begin before the age of thirty. These people pride themselves in self-discipline. One researcher indicates that it is not uncommon for men to retain sexual potency long after the age of seventy. Women play a secondary role to the male and are, for the most part, taught to be dependent on men. Although times are changing there, as well as in America and other countries, many of these traditions are still present. Sexual intercourse is acceptable only after marriage and then it is strictly private. While modern civilization might suggest that this system is inferior to the more "open" atmosphere that is prevalent in many areas of the world, Abkhasians suggest that sex is neither repressed nor evil but is something that should be regulated for the sake of health.

One final reason for the obvious differences between the Abkhasians and other subcultures is their emotional and social security. As one gets older in Abkhasia, he or she is never retired. They are never "put out to pasture" as is so common in other subcultures. From birth to death, they do what they are capable of doing because they believe it to be important to the lives of their fellow citizens. One researcher found that most individuals over one hundred years of age worked an average of four hours a day on a collective farm. While the work was not extremely strenuous, it was necessary and important to the existence of the collective. The elders receive respect from others in their community and feel a need to continue life. As they get older, around one hundred years, they do not feel they are a burden to their family; rather, they feel their family is somewhat dependent on them. In short, they feel needed. Perhaps as Benet suggests, Americans *can* learn something from them!

This is only one example of man's search for immortality. There are others that take place once death has occurred. The hope of returning to consciousness after or between deaths has long been an obsession of man. The Koran suggests that God generates beings and sends them back many times. The Egyptians, who appeared to be more obsessed than other cultures with the concept of immortality, fill their *Book of the Dead* with such sayings as:

> Homage to thee, O Governor, who makest mortals to be born again, who renewest thy youth . . . I am yesterday, today, and tomorrow and I have the power to be born a second time. . . I have knit together my bones; I have made myself whole and sound; I have become young once more; I am Osiris, the Lord of Eternity.[2]

But perhaps ancient Egyptians viewed immortality from a different perspective. Von Daniken, in his question-raising book *Chariots of the Gods*, suggests that various ancient peoples fully understood the techniques of embalming. Did they, in fact, believe in a corporeal return for a second life?

Indeed, the idea of a rebirth is found in the literature of all times and places. In fact, it is suggested that in the unconscious mind, each and every one of us is convinced of our own immortality. We view immortality as an awakening in a life beyond, much in the same way that one wakes up every morning. It is this concern for immortality, for life beyond death, that has enticed man to study that unknown dimension.

Spiritualism

Life after death can be discussed in terms of religion or spiritualism. Actually, the only major difference between conservative religion and spiritualism is the concept of communication. Both believe in life after death. The spiritualist, however, believes that communication between the dead and the living can take place while conservative religions do not.

Spiritualists believe that every living individual has a spirit guide who protects him or her in this life and who prepares us for life after death. In her book, *The Ghosts About Us*, Clara Berke relates her own personal experiences. She claims that the ghosts or spirits of the departed welcome the dying. As her husband was on his deathbed, he commented on the presence of ghosts who looked like his grandmother and mother. He could not understand why his wife could not identify them. While she could not see them, she told her husband that she welcomed them. Berke, offering support of a belief in ghosts, suggests that it is not uncommon for those who are in their final moments to smile, reach out a hand, or call out the name of a deceased loved one.

Spirits, or ghosts, are said to be easily reached if the dead individual was not properly buried, was robbed, or was in any other way mistreated during or after the dying experience. These spirits are said to stay near the earth. If, however, the spirit did not have any of these problems, he ascends to the spirit world. From here, only a very good medium can bridge the communication gap.

Although the concept of ghosts and evil spirits has been with us throughout the ages, spirit rappings in the Fox house in Hydesville, New York in 1848 precipitated the birth of the Spiritualist Movement in the United States. The Fox sisters devised a code for communication with the spirits that consisted of sequences of knocks to identify letters of the alphabet. They began to ask questions that were subsequently answered. Using the alphabet, the sisters were able to decipher messages. Through this code, the Fox sisters were able to learn of a salesman by the name of Charles Rosma who had been murdered by the former owner of the house, John C. Bell. Furthermore, they learned from the spirit of Rosma that he was buried under the house. Later, human bones were unearthed and the rappings in that particular house stopped.

Even though the press and the clergy attacked the "Hydesville Knockings," the Fox sisters had taken up spiritualism as a profession by the end of 1848. Shortly after the Hydesville knockings, rappings reportedly occurred all over the United States. Interest also grew in other countries and it especially increased in England. Seances appeared to be the "in thing" to do. Seances are simply sittings in which any number of people can be involved. A 'medium' is required to serve as a communicative bridge between the sitters and the spirits. It is the purpose of the medium to ask questions of the spirits in such a way that the responses will be intelligible to the sitters. These responses can take either a physical or psychic form. Physical responses include such phenomena as alphabetical rappings in response to questions, table-tipping (movement of the medium's table), or music that is played on instruments by unseen hands. In order for physical responses to take place, the medium need be the only one present. Psychical responses actually occur through the body of the medium. This group of phenomena include such things as clairvoyant visions, writing by the spirit through the medium, and speaking by the spirit through the medium. While there are many forms of spirit communication, those mentioned were the most often used during the early years of spiritualism (the 1850s).

The spiritualist movement continued to grow, claiming millions of followers by the late 1850s. One of the Fox sisters traveled to England in 1871 to intensify an already existing belief in spirits. Then, in 1873, one of the most interesting, historically important phenomena in support of spiritualism occurred. Florence Cook, a medium, was able to bring forth a figure of a woman. Later identified as Katie King, she would walk among and converse with those present at the seance, could be embraced by the sitters, and to the amazement of many, was actually photographed. William Crookes, a scientist holding numerous honorary university degrees and a well-respected man of science, conducted numerous experiments on both Cook and King.

The procedure by which King would appear was simple. Cook would be entranced in a cabinet away from the sitters and King would later appear from within the same cabinet. The normal reaction was that King and Cook were the same person because Cook would not allow anyone to enter the cabinet while she was in the trance. However, Crookes' experiments suggested that this was not the case. In one instance, Crookes took the pulse of Katie King and, a short time later, took that of Miss Cook. The resultant pulses were seventy-five and ninety respectively. Furthermore, Crookes testified after a physical examination of both women that King's heart beat more steadily than Cook's and that King's lungs were sounder than Cook's (Cook was under treatment for a severe cough at the time). While numerous other tests of every conceivable type were utilized, the question of validity rests on the assumption that Crookes was not working *with* Cook rather, he was investigating her. The literature in the years that followed indicates that the latter is not necessarily true. It is proposed that a 'personal relationship' between the two existed and that, in fact, Crookes worked with Cook to deceive the public. Notables of that time, however, indicated the opposite. After reviewing the investigations, such people as Charles Richet, a French physiologist and Nobel prize winner; Rene Sudre, a French writer on parapsychology; and George Zorab, a Dutch parapsychologist; concluded that Crookes was a most respectable man, that his work was founded in scientific procedure, and that there was no reason to doubt his results.

There were religious figures who felt that ministers should relate the story in their sermons. It was believed that the story would indicate proof to people that there is an afterlife. Hence, death was not to be feared.

There are other 'spirit' examples that could be pointed out as they are great in number. Such phenomena are quickly explained away by scientists or sceptics who indicate that while they have not figured out how the mediums use trickery, they someday will. Perhaps they will, but perhaps they may not. What if there is a spirit world? It is not only the task of modern day spiritualists to prove the existence of their beliefs; it is also the task of the scientific community to prove otherwise if they so disbelieve.

Somewhere between the spiritualistic and religious viewpoints is that which we term *life after life*. Actually, it may be "phase one" of the spiritualist movement. It all began with the work of Dr. Russel Noyes, Jr., a psychiatrist at the University of Iowa College of Medicine. Dr. Noyes is cited in the October, 1972 issue of *Psychology Today* for his work with people who have "nearly" died. One such person was Albert Heim, a skilled mountaineer, who fell from a mountain ledge more than seventy feet to a snow covered ledge below. His experience during that fall was recorded in the *Yearbook of the Swiss Alpine Club* around 1891. Hein contacted others who had similar experiences and included these in his report. In his continuing research of such experiences, Noyes has studied the total dying process.

Actually, the dying process can be identified as occurring in one of three general ways. The first can be classified *Sudden Death*, specifically referring to a death that is cognitively unknown to the individual. An example of sudden death would be falling asleep behind the wheel of a car just before the car crashed into a brick wall. In this case, we are assuming that the victim has not awakened at any point and hence, had no cognitive awareness of his impending death. A second type of death can be classified *Sudden-But-Known*. An example of this would be similar to the preceding one, but with the victim awakening at some point during the accident. Hence, the victim in this case has a cognitive awareness of his impending death. The third type of death can be classified *Preconceived Death*. This classification includes those types of death in which the victim has a considerable amount of time to confront his impending death. Terminal illness provides an example of this type of death.

Noyes, in his study of the dying process, has divided the dying experience into three stages or phases. Noyes dealt basically with sudden-but-known types of near death, such as that experienced by Heim. Stage one is labeled "Resistance" and is exemplified by a struggle for survival. Heim reported that as he fell, he surveyed his situation and cognitively planned what to do when he landed. It is suggested that this stage is marked by enormous physical strength as well as increased mental activity. Stage two is entitled "Review" and refers to the victim's review of his or her personal past. In this case, the victim has accepted the fate that lies ahead (death), and he or she reaches a state of tranquility. Frequently reported were cases of "out of the body" experiences. Parapsychologists explain these occurrences by suggesting that the victim's ego splits from his body and watches it act out the past. Experiences range from a few scattered scenes to the entire life of oneself, and from terrifying to peaceful. However, it is noted that the majority are reported to be peaceful. The third stage is termed "Transcendence." Difficult to describe, it is said to be a stage of total awareness. The victim may feel as though he or she were traveling to a previously unknown realm.

Noyes suggested, back in 1972, that understanding this mystical experience could aid the physician in dealing with terminal patients. Utilizing this knowledge, the physician could help take the 'sting' out of death. More recently, Dr. Elisabeth Kubler-Ross has added her support to this concept. In fact, she has gone one step beyond this research. Through her study of terminal illness and active participation in dealing with terminally ill patients, she has reported results similar to Noyes. She claims that she became aware of this phenomenon around 1968 although she was afraid to tell people for fear of ridicule and criticism. She recorded the reactions of those who have undergone clinical death (cessation of respiration and heartbeat) and have later revived. After finding that many of the stories were similar, she began to question the physical and psychological experience of death. Her patients often suggested sensations such as leaving the body and floating above it, beautiful lights, buzzing sounds, and voices of people whom they had known in the past and were now dead. It appears to them as though their spirit or soul has left their body. It then often attempted to communicate with the medical staff trying to inform them that all was well, that death was not bad. Upon failing to communicate, these clinically dead, later revived, individuals reported that their spirit or soul was greeted by someone very close to them who had already died. Additionally, clinically dead patients have been able, after having been revived, to tell such things as who entered the room and what was said during the time that he was showing no heartbeat, pulse, or brainwaves.

Dr. Raymond A. Moody, in his publication *Life After Life*, unknowingly tied the works of Dr. Noyes and Dr. Kubler-Ross together. It should be pointed out that Moody's and Ross' works were done independently of each other. Neither was aware of the other's work until after their findings were on paper. Moody, a physician who has investigated life after death stories (much like Noyes and Kubler-Ross), has extended their work. Stories of about one hundred fifty cases of near death and life after death experiences were recorded. Such experiences can be categorized into three types of phenomena:

1. Those who were clinically dead (and/or thought to be so)
2. Those who came close to death
3. Those who related stories as they were dying

Rather than looking at these as three separate categories of experiences, Moody notes that all three contain some similar elements. Hence, the three categories are really part of a life through death continuum. Note the diagram below:

| Life | Close to Death type Experience | Dying Experiences | Clinical Death | Death |

The closer one gets to the death end of the continuum before returning to life, the more complete and colorful the experience. Some stages, and events throughout this process are commonly reported. Noyes, Kubler-Ross, and Moody all suggest various events that occur in some order, but Moody's work is perhaps the most detailed. Pulling all of their work together, we can identify the common elements as one passes from the "life" to the "death" end of the continuum.

1. The first common element occurs when one is pronounced, either by bystanders or by a physician, dead. The victim, in many cases, hears this pronouncement.
2. Feelings of relief, peace, quiet, and lack of pain follow the pronouncement of death.
3. Sounds of buzzing or ringing are next. More often than not, these sounds are reported as pleasant but some victims later relate these sounds as harsh or unpleasant.
4. Occurring almost at the same time as the sound, victims report that they are drawn into a void or tunnel that is absent of light, yet they can somehow see or feel the presence of the void as they are able, in some cases, to describe it.
5. After passing through this tunnel or void, the victims are able to see themselves because they are now outside of their bodies. They can see their physical bodies lying on the street following an accident, or lying on an operating or emergency room table with physicians working on them. They have, at this point, no physical feelings. The "spirit" body of which they are now part can pass through solid objects because it is not solid.

6. From the experiences of those who have passed yet closer to the "death" end of the continuum, many report that they saw and met with people they formally knew or in some cases, with new acquaintances. These new acquaintances were described as spirits who were sent to help or guide them. The victims could communicate with the spirits but it was usually the figure that did the talking.

7. Moving closer to death, the victim can see a light that is very bright, yet he is able to look at it without pain. It is not an offensive bright light. He gets closer and closer to it but it does not hurt. Descriptions of the light vary from "Christ" to "an angel" to "a being of light." Interpretation appears to be related to the victim's religious background. They could communicate with the "being" (which took human form), but did so without talking. The being would ask the victim questions about his or her life and accomplishments. These questions would lead the victim into the next event.

8. Following a meeting with "the light," the victim would confront a review of his life. Although the accounts vary, most victims maintain that they can see the more important parts of their lives pass before them as though on a panoramic screen.

9. Finally, the victim who passes closest to the "death" end of the continuum, approaches a border type of experience. Again, described in different ways, the concept is basically that the victim believes he will surely be dead if he passes over this border. In almost all cases reported by Moody, the victim is turned around and does not pass over this line.

10. Most victims report that they, in fact, do not wish to return to their bodies. The peace and tranquility that they have found is pleasant, more pleasant than the life they must return to. However, they have no choice. They are returned, against their will, to their bodies.

Moody's results clarify the sketchy work of Noyes and Kubler-Ross. All together, they paint a rather vivid picture of what goes on as one approaches total death, which is surely somewhere beyond clinical death. Of course other explanations for these phenomena are proposed by various professionals but because the elements mentioned are "common" and Noyes, Kubler-Ross, and Moody "independently" concluded similar elements after researching those who had undergone the experience, these are, indeed, intriguing facts. Perhaps their "life after death" hypothesis has its basis in fact. It surely does not disavow any known religion; it apparently supports almost all of them.

Cryonics

Although not a spiritual or religious concept of life after death, cryonics also offers the same long-sought goal: immortality. The word *cryonics* comes from the Greek *cryos*, which means *icy cold*. Today's meaning of the word cryonics is *the storage or preservation of human bodies by low temperature technology.* The concept proposes that those dying of a terminal disease may be frozen until the time when medical technology can supply an answer or cure for their illness. At that time, the body will be thawed, life will begin again, and the previous terminal disease will be cured. This concept became a reality as a result of Robert C.W. Ettinger and his interest in cryobiology (low temperature biology). Recovering from a Second World War wound in 1947, he reportedly read the work of Jean Rostand who had successfully frozen and thawed frog sperm. Ettinger immediately saw the implications of this work for humans. It was from this early interest, and his publication of *The Prospect of Immortality* in 1962, that the groundwork for cryonic suspension was laid.

At the present time, because of concerns regarding euthanasia and mercy killing, the patient must be clinically dead prior to subjection of the freezing process. This is far from ideal since cellular damage occurs up to the time of clinical death. It would seem far superior for the freezing process to be initiated prior to clinical death. This would result in fewer difficulties once the individual is thawed. Presently, however, the body is immediately put on ice following clinical death. This retards further cell damage until cryonic specialists can obtain the body. This 'icing' stage is bypassed if cryonic specialists can be at the scene of the death. This may occur in a hospital when death is expected.

Once obtained, the blood from the body is drained and a protective chemical solution composed mainly of glycerol is circulated throughout the body. This minimizes further damage to the cells during further steps. Once this process, called perfusion, is completed, the body is wrapped in aluminum foil for protection against accumulated frost due to condensation. It is then stored in a dry ice container similar in appearance to a coffin at a temperature of around −79°C. From this temporary icebox, the body is then transferred to a capsule that is constructed much like a thermos bottle. The capsule is filled with liquid nitrogen, which lowers the body temperature to −196°C. (−320°F). Molecular movement ceases. At this temperature (for all practical purposes), cellular deterioration is arrested. Liquid nitrogen must be replenished on a regular basis. The capsule is not dependent on electricity in any way. Hence, the fear of future electrical "blackouts" or shortages is eliminated.

No, cryonics is not a thing of the future. It does not come out of some science fiction story, although it may well be a science fiction concept. It is a realistic alternative to immediate death. Various organic substances have been successfully frozen or near-frozen and thawed later with minimal cellular damage. Cryobiological advances indicate that living tissue can survive the process of freezing. Almost every type of mammalian tissue has been successfully frozen and likewise thawed.

Sperm, frozen for several years, has been used later in artificial insemi-nation. Skin, corneas, and bone marrow are frozen in liquid nitrogen and used later for grafting. Medical advances like these continue to astonish the skeptic. But advancement in cryonic suspension does not stop here. Dr. Paul Segall, a physiologist at the University of California, has successfully placed mice and hamsters in hypothermic suspended animation for several hours. During this time span there was no re-corded heartbeat. The animals were resuscitated and revived. In another experiment, Dr. Isamu Suda, of Kobe University in Japan, froze the brain of a cat for more than six months at −20°C. Upon thawing, the cat's brain demonstrated near-normal brain wave patterns.

Recently, Dr. Keith Miller of the Institute of Arctic Biology in Alaska demonstrated that Arctic beetles can be frozen to temperatures of −87°C. and survive. Interestingly, the body fluids of these insects con-tain glycerol which is similar to the solution used in human cryonic suspension.

Finally, three Soviet scientists have cryonically suspended dead rabbits to temperatures a few degrees above freezing. Upon thawing, the scientists discovered that most of the rabbits' biological functions resumed. The rabbits were, for all practical purposes, once again alive.

The first human was cryonically suspended in 1967. He was Dr. James Bedford, a Ph.D. in psychology. He died of terminal cancer and was immediately suspended in his frozen environment. Since then, many more have been suspended. Some have even been thawed and buried due to a 'change of heart' on the part of the family. As of January, 1976 twenty-six people remain suspended. A human has never gone through the entire process; therefore, investigation of human bodily functions after thawing has never been complete.

Various cryonics societies exist including the Bay Area Cryonics Society in Oakland, California and the New York Cryonics Society in Long Island, New York. Other organizations and societies active in the cryonics movement exist in Appleton, Wisconsin; Costa Mesa, Califor-nia; Oak Park, Michigan; North Miami, Florida; San Diego, California; Paris, France; Australia, and Austria. A fee of one thousand dollars, paid only once, is charged for membership in one of these societies. This fee helps to provide operational capital. All members who wish to be cryon-ically suspended wear Medic Alert bracelets that ambulance drivers, policemen, firemen, and doctors look for in emergency cases. The bracelet has a phone number inscribed on it that medical personnel may contact in case of accidental death. Cryonic specialists will be on the scene as soon as possible to cryonically suspend the member. Additionally, all members carry a cryonics alert card that directs those in charge, in the case of death of the card holder, to wrap the body in ice and have it shipped to a local cryonics unit. There it will be frozen and placed in a capsule.

Sound terribly simple? In truth, it is not. Those interested are informed that they should purchase a fifty thousand dollar life insurance policy. About fifteen thousand dollars is set aside for the purchase of the capsule and the initial freezing. The remaining thirty-five thousand dollars is placed in a trust and actually earns interest each year for that eventual day when you return. Maintenance of the capsule, which costs about eighteen hundred dollars a year, is paid off by the interest. Whatever remains is transferred back to the cryonically suspended individual when he is thawed. Cryonic societies have arranged policies like the one above with a large insurance firm today. However, with inflation, one might wish to have more money waiting when he "returns."

While the process itself may sound simple, keep in mind that the knowledge of techniques or procedures regarding the thawing process is still lacking. The hope is that eventually, future medical technology will bring with it the answers. Actually, we have little reason to doubt such a belief. Looking at medical advancement during the past fifty years, such an advanced procedure does not seem beyond the scope of reality. It is also hoped that medical technology will bring with it the answer for the cause of death of the suspended individual. This is also not unthinkable. Continuing research will surely lead to cures for many human afflictions. Heart disease, cancer, even old age may someday be curable. That 'someday' may be sooner than many of us think.

Ideally, freezing an individual *before* death would make this individual a more perfect candidate for cryonic suspension. However, a person *must* be declared legally dead and legal death occurs when the physician says it does. But cells of the dead body continue to live. Even after clinical death, almost all of a patient's cells are still alive. Additionally, arrangements for suspension should be made through a lawyer rather than through the family. It is not uncommon for a family member to alter the wishes of the deceased.

Here are some final thoughts that legal authorities are going to have to face. What if one were married, his wife died, and he had her frozen? Would he marry again? Legally, could he marry again? What if *he* was cryonically suspended ten years later? Upon thawing both people, would they still be married? If he had married again and his second wife was still alive, would he be a bigamist? The Cryonics Society of New York has its lawyers working, trying to resolve such questions and change current laws. In the *Prospect of Immortality*, Ettinger offers solutions to many of the religious, social, and moral questions that arise.

Meanwhile, actual participation in the Cryonics movement has reportedly declined. Perhaps this is because of lack of support from the scientific community. But most likely, it is the failure of the scientific community to educate the public regarding the advances made in this area. Second, many people wish to have all of the answers 'now'. Hence, interest has declined not only from the lack of educational measures on behalf of the medical-scientific community, but from lack of patience on behalf of 'semibelievers'.

Regardless, cryonics must be considered an alternative to immediate death as it offers the hope of immortality. Remember the old adage, "You can't take your money with you." If you invest in the "possibility" of living once again and science is unable to develop those techniques required for successful thawing, the worst that could happen is that you would still be dead.

SUMMARY

Man is the only animal capable of understanding his inevitable death. He is also the only animal that shows any signs of doubt regarding its eventuality. His concern with immortality is abundant in the literature of all times and places. From the Abkhasians, who extend their life expectancy through a number of factors, to the spiritualists and theologians, immortality appears to be a primary concern. Spiritualists and theologians both perceive a life after death with the main difference between the two being that spiritualists believe in possible communication with those in the other world (spirits or souls).

Noyes, Kubler-Ross, and Moody have collected and disseminated data suggesting similar stages or phases that an individual goes through as he approaches irreversible death. Their work gives some credibility to the concept of life after death.

Cryonics, freezing the body at or near death for thawing out at a later date when science can solve the problem or illness that caused death, is man's most recent attempt to create a science of immortality.

NOTES

1. William Ernest Hocking, *The Meaning of Immortality In Human Experience* (New York: Harper and Brothers, 1957), p. 5.

2. Alan Harrington, *The Immortalist* (New York: Random House, 1969), p. 27.

<hr>

———————————— **SELECTED BIBLIOGRAPHY** ————

BENET, SULA, "Why They Live To Be 100, Or Even Older, In Abkhasia," *Readings In Health*, pp. 45–51. Guilfor, Connecticut: Duskin Publishing Group, Inc., 1976.

BERKE, CLARA, *The Ghosts About Us*. Philadelphia, Pennsylvania: Dorrance and Company, 1969.

"Cryonics: Answers To The Most Frequently Asked Questions," pp. 9–10. Pamphlet. Berkeley, California: Trans Time, Inc., 1975.

DANIEL, GLENDA, "Evidence Convinces Psychiatrist There Is Life After Death," *Chicago Tribune*, November 18, 1975, sec. 3, p. 3, col. 1.

ETTINGER, ROBERT C. W., *The Prospect of Immortality*. New York: Doubleday and Company, 1964.

HALL, TREVOR H., *New Light On Old Ghosts*. London: Gerald Duckworth and Co., Ltd., 1965.

HALL, TREVOR H., *The Spiritualist*. New York: Helix Press, 1963.

HARRINGTON, ALAN, *The Immortalist*, p. 27. New York: Random House, 1969.

HENDIN, DAVID, *Death As A Fact Of Life*, pp. 163–64. New York: Warner Paperback Library, 1974.

HOCKING, WILLIAM ERNEST, *The Meaning of Immortality In Human Experience*, p. 5. New York: Harper and Brothers, 1957.

"Immortality: A Possible Dream," *Pageant*, 30, no. 7 (January 1975), 57.

KERR, HOWARD, *Mediums, and Spirit Rappers, and Roaring Radicals*. Urbana, Illinois: University of Illinois Press, 1972.

NELSON, ROBERT F. AND SANDRA STANLEY, *We Froze the First Man*. New York: Dell Paperback, 1968.

"The Outlook," *Bulletin of the Cryonics Society of Michigan*, 6, no. 1 (1975).

ROSENFELD, ALBERT, *The Second Genesis*. Englewood Cliffs, New Jersey: Prentice-Hall, Inc., 1969.

SCHULTZ, DODI, "The Verdict on Vitamins," *Readings In Health*, p. 83. Guilfor, Connecticut: Duskin Publishing Group, Inc., 1976.

VON DANIKEN, ERICH, *Chariots of the Gods?* p. 80. New York: Bantam Books, Inc., 1969.

WRIGHT, THEON, *The Open Door*. New York: The John Day Company, 1970.

11

In the Last Analysis

'Oh, God, if I was sure I were to die tonight I would repent at once.' It is the commonest prayer in all languages.

(J. M. BARRIE)

In the last analysis, it is our concern with life that distorts our perspective of death. Through a variety of avoidance techniques we have successfully displaced most thoughts of death. Instead of death being a part of growth and life, it is often regarded as that which is to be ignored. In almost all other areas of concern, the end is the final product. In life, the end is regarded as unfortunate or catastrophic. Hence, everyone considers death an undesirable goal. When something is considered undesirable, we attempt to protect other members of society from it. As such, we place the dying in hospitals or other such environments. Rather than learn from the dying patient, we strip him of his dignity and allow him to die alone in a sterile environment. We choose to remain ignorant regarding his feelings and attitudes. A few researchers, including Dr. Elisabeth Kubler-Ross, have struck out in protest. These researchers have suggested that we can, in fact, learn from the dying. To learn what is cold, we must learn what is hot. Is it not also logical that to learn about life, we must be aware of what death is?

Some suggest that we do not need to study death. They suggest that we never needed it before; consequently, we do not need it now. The only response to this group is that times are changing. In earlier days, death was a family event. All were involved and all learned from it. This is no longer the case. Death, as mentioned before, is removed from the family environment under the auspices that we are being "protected" from this unfortunate end.

Our attitudes are founded on the basis of past philosophical, religious, and cultural thought. Socrates, Plato, Aristotle, and Heidegger, among other philosophers, gave meaning to life through their separate interpretations of death. Christians, Jews, Moslems, Hindus, Eskimos, and American Indians are among various religious and cultural groups who attempt to add meaning to life through the discovery and examination of death. If one is a part of that religious or cultural group, surely his attitude toward death is greatly affected by it. As one becomes more comfortable with the death concept, so will he become more comfortable with life itself.

In a preceding chapter of this book, it was suggested that *some* attitudinal studies have been undertaken with *some* age groups within the United States. It should be pointed out that this is not strictly an American phenomenon. Other countries throughout the world have also undertaken studies to examine attitudes toward death.

The basic concept underlying death education is "honesty." The majority of problems related to children and death stem from an inconsistent response pattern from meaningful adults. The child hears one explanation from one adult and a different explanation from another adult. It does not take too long before a child figures out that he is being lied to. This is wrong, even under the auspices of protection.

One concern underlying the concept of honesty is that of participation. If you are honest with a child and explain what has happened regarding a death, you may allow him to participate in the funerary process if he so desires. It is incorrect to force him to participate, but if he would like to, you should cooperate. Both honesty and voluntary participation will allow the child to accept the death and form a more favorable future concept of death.

The process of death is indeed difficult to pinpoint or define. There is little reason to doubt that during the 1900s the fear of premature burial was a reality. Even today, rare as it may seem, we hear of someone who has reportedly died only to awaken on the embalmer's table. With all of today's technology, mistakes are still made. All that can be expected is a reduction in the number of those mistakes. Embalming in this country has somewhat removed the fear of premature burial. The current movement to continuously redefine death has occurred as a result of transplantation rather than fear of premature burial. Even with the most widely accepted standards for defining death as put forth by the Harvard University Committee, we should not be too quick to discount the experience of the physician. Rather than search and work for a "legal" definition, we should put more faith in the clinical judgement of the physician. The court, at the present time, cannot possibly draw up a set of standards that applies to *all* deaths. Faith in the physician implies that he, from past experience and availability of medical resources, is able to make the best decision. Faith in the physician implies that he is not going to produce your death if there is any hope of life just so he can utilize one or many of your organs to help others live. It is often difficult to have faith in that which you do not understand. But the choice is not a simple one. Either you have faith in medical technology and the physician or you have faith in the legal institutions. Actually, we are most fortunate at the present time since the legal authorities have little say over a definition of death, yet they do watch over medical authorities.

Whatever the definition or diagnosis, transplantation has become a viable alternative to impending death for many. It would be next to impossible to estimate the number of people who are alive today as a result of transplants. Statistically, some transplants are far more successful than others. However, even the most unsuccessful offer a chance for life. Transplants are dependent on donors, i.e., those who accept their own inevitable deaths and make plans for their body parts. This is basically where the problem lies. Most of us cannot accept our deaths, or we believe death will happen when we are very old. Hence, we believe we have time before making plans for donation. We do not believe that we may go out after finishing this chapter and die within minutes or hours. The author believes that everyone should send for, obtain, and fill out a donor's card now if it does not interfere with your personal or religious beliefs. The gift you leave behind will be remembered by few; no one will pat you on the back and congratulate you for what a kind person you are; you probably will not even know the person whose life you may save. Yet, your gift is the greatest one that you have to offer, the gift of life.

> Pray that your loneliness may spur you into finding
> something to live for, great enough to die for.

> (DAG HAMMARSKJOLD)

The will to live is not only a subconscious thought, it is also a physical reality. The human body often does things that many believe it incapable of doing. Physical stresses of old age are met head-on and fought. Eventually, the mind and the body are defeated but they often do much to delay this defeat. Medical science is helping the mind and the body delay death. Some believe that we may eventually "cure" death. While others do not believe this, they do accept the fact that medical science will someday be able to prolong life far beyond what is 'normal' today. It is necessary that one keep this concept in perspective. Quantity is not always better than quality. Note the following:

> Whoever has lived long enough to find out what life is knows
> how deep a debt of gratitude we owe to Adam, the first great
> benefactor of our race. He brought death into the world.

> (MARK TWAIN)

Perhaps Twain's reaction was built upon society's neglect and general nonacceptance of the elderly. Our culture is guilty of emphasizing youth and de-emphasizing the elderly. We can learn much from the older members of our society, yet we place them aside and disregard them. This is a truly unfortunate aspect of our culture. However, this may be slowly changing because of many factors. Various organizations, committees, and subcommittees have turned their attention to that productive segment of our society known as the elderly. But until it does change, that older segment can look forward to traditional problems. What will they do all day? Where will they live? How will they live? Options such as part-time jobs can help them feel useful. The choice of a nursing home is often less than desirable; however, many do not even have that choice. If they have not saved enough money for retirement, they must try to live on welfare and social security. The painted picture is not all that pretty. We should all reassess our own attitudes toward the elderly. Why do we feel the way we do? Try to imagine yourself as an older, retired member of society. What do *you* expect? If you live long enough, you may develop some fatal, degenerative, terminal disease or disorder. Would you like to have knowledge of this disease or disorder kept from you? Opinions on this question vary as do the reactions once one is told. If, during your lifetime, you have developed an acceptant attitude toward death, knowledge of a terminal disease or disorder may come as no surprise or threat. After all, you expect to die. You have accepted that fact and knowing it will happen soon should only prompt you to get on with living out your final days as you so desire.

Hospices can help you live out those days when it gets too difficult to care for oneself. They allow a person the dignity of life as well as the dignity of death. However, they are almost nonexistent in this country. Again, there seems to be a prevailing attitude in our culture that death should not be accepted, that it should be avoided or prolonged at almost all cost. Interestingly, the elderly do not fear death as much as they fear the manner in which they will die. Perhaps this reveals something about traditional medical facilities for the elderly versus the hospice.

As for your reactions to a dying patient, one would do well to understand Ross' five stages that terminally ill patients may pass through. Understanding these stages can offer one the knowledge of how to act and what to expect from the patient. It is through this understanding that help for the patient as well as for yourself can be achieved. Understanding can eliminate ignorance and make the process of adaptation less difficult. For example, understanding the sudden infant death syndrome helps one realize the trauma that parents of a SIDS victim undergo. In this still unexplained mystery, the parents need not feel guilt or shame. In other words, nothing that they could have done would have avoided the final outcome. Again understanding can help free one of guilt, shame, or a multitude of other reactions. It helps one realize the inevitability of life and death, and in doing so, helps one to react accordingly.

> Many men would take the death-sentence without a whimper
> to escape the life-sentence which fate carries in her
> other hand.
>
> (T. E. Lawrence)

Is it possible, as Lawrence suggests, that death may actually be better than life under some circumstances? The questions of euthanasia and suicide will no doubt perplex us in the future as it has in the past. We look to the courts for answers but the courts are of little help. Euthanasia centers (as in the movie *Soilent Green*) may well be a thing of the future. Surely most of us fear the possibility of mass genocide (euthanasia for genetic or political undesirables). But this is a far cry from the movement for legalization of euthanasia as it exists today. Arguments both for and against euthanasia have been with us before, are with us now, and will be with us in the future. Still, is it not the right of every human being to refuse medical care? Is not the pain of perpetual life on a machine worse than the sting of death for many? Both the Society for the Right to Die and the Euthanasia Educational Council answer *yes!* Physicians reportedly tend to agree. Legally, however, euthanasia is not widely accepted. The "Living Will" has not yet been tested in a court of law. Legal authorities, while not passing laws in favor of euthanasia, appear to have accepted the concept by rarely charging a physician with murder, even though some have outwardly admitted to the practice. Morally, we have accepted the concept of suicide as well. Where we used to think of it as a crime, we are now more concerned with the person, and rightly so. A wealth of material has been published over the last ten years on suicide. We now have many different formulas to predict suicide potential. Additionally, we have many different organizations to help a potential suicide victim. In reality, we cannot stop the three to five percent who really wish to succeed. But, perhaps for them, the pain of life is worse than the pain or thought of death. Let us not be so quick to judge that which we cannot comprehend.

> The god-men say when die go sky/Through Pearly Gates where
> river flow,/The god-men say when die we fly/Just like eagle-
> hawk and crow-/Might be, might-be; but I don't know.

> (ANONYMOUS)

After death, dependent on the culture, there are a series of processes or procedures that must ritualistically be carried out. These rituals are indicative of the concept of death and the possibility of life after death. They usually begin when the victim is about to die and proceed for a specific time period (years in some cultures) after the burial. Interestingly, we tend to show more respect for the newly dead than we do for the living.

> I never heard him say much in favour of the absent living,
> but, a charitable man, he always spoke well of the dead.

> (DOMINIC BEHAN)

Burial requirements tend to differ, even within the same culture, depending on the geographical location of the people involved. The easiest method of disposal of a body in a particular environment is usually the most preferred method of the masses. Laws governing body disposal reflect the values that the particular culture holds (or held in the immediate past).

Gifts of some form are given either for burial with the dead or are given to the family of the deceased. Dressing of the dead, type of coffin used (if any), preparation of the body for burial, and religious services are all entrenched in sometimes unwritten rituals.

While atypical in other countries, embalming is almost a regular practice in the United States. Embalmers are professionally trained at certified institutions of higher education. Their professional training enables them not only to embalm the corpse but to serve a funerary function for the bereaved.

After preparation of the body, disposal can take many forms varying from burial underground to burial on top of the ground, and from cremation to sea burial. Again, the desired method of the culture is usually dependent on the geographical location of that culture. For example, cremation and sea burial is far more common in California than it is in Illinois. Cremation in the United States is slowly becoming a preferred method of body disposal. The major reason is probably based on its inexpensiveness when compared to the traditional burial process. Religious taboos against cremation have been withdrawn over the centuries, and today it is a viable alternative.

A movement to promote cremation began in the late 1800s. At that time, there was a fear among many regarding a dead body and the possibility of the spread of disease. Today, perhaps a more realistic rationale exists. The preservation of land is a concern that has gained much support in the United States. What better way to conserve needed land space than to promote cremation?

Today, burial at sea is just an extension of the cremation process, i.e., the cremated remains are scattered at sea. This was not always the case. It used to be that sea burial implied disposition of the entire body into the waters of the sea. This is rarely done today.

Various organizations now exist for the purpose of sea burial and/or cremation throughout the United States. These organizations tend to be in disagreement with the funeral home-cemetery complex about *which* is the better service. This is realistic in that both are competitors competing for the right to serve people in a time of need. All things considered, there is room for both types of organizations. Eventually, all of us will see one or the other.

Approximately seventy percent of the thirty churches referred to in this text approve of cremation. Seven percent actually prefer cremation to any other form of body disposition. Even in the case of those twenty-three percent who disapprove of cremation, they are not opposed to it in cases involving communicable diseases for sanitary purposes. Clearly, the trend toward cremation is slowly increasing throughout the world.

Religious authorities look more favorably toward the prospect of body or body part donation for the purpose of transplantation. Ninety percent of the religions find both practices either acceptable or one of individual decision. Quite a few religions actually encourage such practices while some are careful to qualify their positions. The Buddhist Churches of America find body or body part donation an acceptable practice 'in some situations'. The Greek Orthodox Church accepts body part donations but not the donation of the entire body. Jehovah's Witnesses forbid any type of donation while the followers of Judaism are requested to discuss the matter with their rabbi as the decision-making procedure is quite complex. Basically, most churches support the concept that the gift of one's body or body parts, as a final act of life, is humanitarian because it is done so that others might live. The only question of concern is how such donation affects the quality and length of the donor's life.

The churches of the world are not nearly as acceptant of euthanasia as they are of cremation or donation. Only thirty percent of these churches declare the practice of euthanasia as either acceptable or one of individual decision. The majority (sixty-three percent) maintain that euthanasia is an unacceptable practice. Only two churches, the Mennonite Church and the Roman Catholic Church, make a distinction between what we have labeled euthanasia and mercy killing. While both find euthanasia an acceptable practice, both also condemn mercy killing and view it as an unacceptable practice. It is perhaps interesting to note that the vast majority of churches make no such distinction.

> When I die people will say it is the best thing for me. It is because they know it is the worst. They want to avoid the feeling of pity. As though they were the people most concerned.
>
> (IVY COMPTON-BURNETT)

Bereavement is a generalized illness that occurs as a result of the breakage of the social and emotional bonds between two people. Although we typically discuss bereavement in terms of death, we can identify the bereavement process throughout life at times such as divorce or forced separation.

Especially important is the understanding that bereavement affects all three dimensions of the human, i.e., the physical, mental-emotional, and social dimensions. Hence, it is not simply a physical disorder for which one must see a physician; it is not simply a mental-emotional disorder for which one must see a psychiatrist; nor is it simply a social disorder that can be treated by sensitivity groups or others in the same predicament. It is a complex problem that has its basis in all three dimensions. Fortunately, in most cases, it is self-correcting. Most of us will inevitably adapt to the death of a loved one. Some, however, will not. They may demonstrate atypical or abnormal grief reactions and, in doing so, indicate the need for grief therapy.

The role of the funeral and subsequent rituals is believed by most authorities in the bereavement field to play an important role in repairing the emotional and social damage that death has caused. The funeral and its rituals allow the bereaved to socially display expected and necessary reactions. The bereaved benefit in the short run, and society as a whole benefits in the long run.

The duration of time regarding bereavement varies from individual to individual and is probably dependent on the intensity of one's social and emotional ties to the deceased. To more effectively shorten the bereavement time, some individuals suggest that it is important to spend more money than you can comfortably afford on the funeral.

> 'There is no death,' she said. 'No, my dear lady,
> but there are funerals.'
>
> (PETER DE VRIES)

Today, funeral directors can easily rip off the consumer. This has happened in the past and it will more than likely happen in the future; however, it is the consumer who most often rips off himself. He desires, and in many cases requires, an expensive funeral. It makes him feel better and helps him adapt to the death. As his desires or requirements increase, so also must the cost of the funeral. If one were to shop around (which one does not usually do in a time of grief and mourning), he could find an inexpensive solution to the problem of a dignified disposal of the deceased. But if we require all types of services and a quality-built, airtight, waterproof casket (that may slow decomposition), we must pay for it.

If slow decomposition or immortality is what you desire, consider the method of cryonics.

> Stirring suddenly from long hibernation/I knew myself
> once more a poet/Guarded by timeless principalities/
> Against the worm of death.
>
> (ROBERT GRAVES)

Cryonic suspension, for all practical purposes, halts cellular decomposition. In one's search for immortality, it is the only alternative based on scientific principles at the present time. Belief in spirits or ghosts is another alternative. Although the body dies, in essence, the soul does not.

> My soul looked down from a vague height with
> Death/As unremembering how I rose or why/And
> saw a sad land, weak with sweats of dearth.
>
> (WILFRED OWEN)

In the selection of either one, we have chosen an alternative to the concept that death ends all. If we firmly believe in one of these, then death will hold no terror. Even if you do not believe in immortality in any sense, death should not seem frightening or terrible. As Stevie Smith suggests,

> I do really think that death will be marvelous....
> If there wasn't death, I think you couldn't go on.

12

What About
a Will?

Although a will is not necessary in *all* cases, those exceptions that are unpredictable make it a modern-day requirement. It may well be one of the most important documents that you can prepare for the insurance of your survivors' protection. As such, there are a number of reasons supportive of writing a will. There are really no reasons for *not* writing a will. So, while it may not always be necessary, depending on your social position and life-role, it would rarely be detrimental. The only negative aspect might be signing a valid will, deciding to change it at a later date, but forgetting or being unable to do so.

Reasons supportive of writing a will can best be summarized by the following points:

1. You can arrange to give what you want to whom you want.
2. It may reduce the "fights" over your property among your relatives and/or friends.
3. It may reveal certain aspects of your financial affairs that are unknown to those concerned.
4. It affords you the opportunity to select a guardian for any children surviving you.
5. It will minimize certain estate handling costs.
6. You can declare any charities to whom you may wish to donate money or personal belongings.
7. You can set up conditions with which your children or beneficiaries must comply in order to obtain your bequests.

While these seven points summarize the advantages of writing a will, they by no means exhaust them. There are other advantages that are less apparent.

Simply defined, a will is a legal document that takes effect at the time of death of the writer and that designates how his or her property is to be disposed of. Up until the time of death a person may revoke, rewrite, or amend his will.

While there are six specific types of wills, only the last one mentioned here is recommended for use. The reasoning behind this will become evident as we look at each.

1. Nuncupative Will: *Nuncupative* literally means oral rather than written. While this type of will is not legally binding in many states, it is sometimes accepted in some areas or states in certain emergency situations (a soldier at war, a sailor at sea, or any person finding himself threatened by immediate death). Even in cases where it is considered binding, the person must have two witnesses. The factors surrounding this type of will make its use limited as well as generally undesirable.

2. Holographic Will: *Holographic* is defined as totally in the handwriting of the testator (will-maker). It does not require attestation by witnesses. However, it is also not legally binding in most of the fifty United States.

3. Joint Will: A joint will is a combined effort of two or more people. Hence, a husband and wife may sign a joint will, but unless there is a special provision written into it, it legally binds the two together. As such, if one dies first, the other may not change or revoke the will.

4. Mutual Will: Mutual wills are like joint wills, but they have what is called a "reciprocal provision." Each party signing the will leaves everything to the other person or partner. (Individual states have different legal policies in handling joint and mutual wills. It is recommended that legal guidance be sought in your state.)

5. Conditioned Wills: This type of will usually describes an event that must occur after the testator's death before the will becomes valid. There are many stories of people who, afraid of being buried alive, would describe certain procedures to assure their death before burial. Only after these procedures were followed would their will become valid. There are various problems associated with this type of will. For example, when a gift is conditioned upon an act of the beneficiary that in "good" morals should not be so conditioned, the gift may be declared invalid. Hence, depending on a court decision, you may not be able to condition your gift dependent on the beneficiary changing his religion or "until he marries." Generally speaking, the gift of the testator cannot be tied up for an indefinite period of time. In the United States, this period of time is usually one generation, i.e., about thirty years.

6. Conventional Will: This will is the one will that most readily stands up in a court of law. States differ in their requirements (some may require an exact form to be used). While this will is not too complicated to make, it does require the assistance of a legal representative.

Generally, the testator must be at least eighteen years old, the will must be in writing, and it must be signed in the presence of at least two witnesses.

Of the six types of wills, only the last is highly recommended. It is apparent that one should not draft a will without legal advice. Furthermore, it is advised that you have your will regularly checked with a lawyer because your life-style may change.

SUMMARY

Because we tend to avoid thoughts of death, we tend to avoid the subject of writing wills. It must be understood that if we die without a will, we lose all power to determine how our property will be handled. Without a will, our property becomes the property of the state, which, in effect, will write a will for us. The state will, by preestablished laws, determine the handling of our estate.

All wills should be handled by competent lawyers to avoid confusion, fights, and legal problems over your estate. Utilizing lawyers is not an inexpensive venture, but considering the possible problems over your estate and your desire to take care of your family in the best way possible, it is not an expensive venture either.

Appendices

APPENDIX A

Addresses of Organizations Responsive to Thanatological Concerns

ACS/NIH Organ Transplant
Registry
55 East Erie Street
Chicago, Illinois 60611

American Medical Association
535 North Dearborn Street
Chicago, Illinois 60610

Ars Moriendi
7301 Huron Lane
Philadelphia, Pennsylvania 19119

Bay Area Cryonics Society, Inc.
2555 Leimert Boulevard
Oakland, California 94602

Cryo Era Corporation and Hope
Knoll Cemetery Association
c/o Joseph Cannon
2515 Gmeiner Road
Appleton, Wisconsin 54911

Cryonics Society of Australia
c/o Tony Keulemans
P.O. Box 18
Oconnor ACT 3601
Australia

Cryonics Society of Austria
II Hauptplatz
2620 Neunkierchen N.-O
Austria

Cryonics Society of California
P.O. Box 2292
Costa Mesa, California 92626

Cryonics Society of France
10 Rue Thiboumery
Paris 15, France

Cryonics Society of Michigan
24041 Stratford
Oak Park, Michigan 48237

Cryonics Society of New York
9 Holmes Court
Sayville, Long Island
New York 11782

Cryonics Society of San Diego
4791 50th Street
San Diego, California 92115

Cryonics Society of South Florida
P.O. Box 693
North Miami, Florida 33161

Euthanasia Educational Council
250 West 57th Street
New York, New York 10019

Eye-Bank Association of America
3195 Maplewood Avenue
Winston-Salem, North Carolina
27103

Eye-Bank for Sight Restoration,
Inc.
210 East 64th Street
New York, New York 10021

Forum for Death Education and
Counseling, Inc.
P.O. Box 1226
Arlington, Virginia 22210

Foundation for the Advancement
of Medical Knowledge
21 East 90th Street
New York, New York 10028

Foundation of Thanatology
630 West 168th Street
New York, New York 10032

Hospice, Inc.
765 Prospect Street
New Haven, Connecticut 06511

National Association of Patients
  on Hemodialysis and
  Transplantation
P.O. Box 60
Brooklyn, New York 11203

National Funeral Directors
  Association
135 West Wells Street
Milwaukee, Wisconsin 53203

National Kidney Foundation, Inc.
315 Park Avenue South
New York, New York 10010

Neptune Society
680 Beach, Suite 451
San Francisco, California 94101

Telophase Society
1333 Camino Del Rio South
San Diego, California 92108

Trans-Time, Inc.
1122 Spruce Street
Berkeley, California 94707

APPENDIX B

IMPORTANT: Do not read these pages unless you have finished this book.

Death Attitude Scale: Post-Test

The following items are not intended to test your knowledge. There are
no right or wrong answers. Your responses are anonymous. Directions:
Read each item carefully. Place a check mark next to each item with
which you *Agree.* Make *No Marks* next to items with which you disagree.

249_____The thought of death is a glorious thought.
247_____When I think of death I am most satisfied.
245_____Thoughts of death are wonderful thoughts.
243_____The thought of death is very pleasant.
241_____The thought of death is comforting.
239_____I find it fairly easy to think of death.
237_____The thought of death isn't so bad.
235_____I do not mind thinking of death.
233_____I can accept the thought of death.
231_____To think of death is common.
229_____I don't fear thoughts of death, but I don't like them
either.
227_____Thinking about death is over-valued by many.
225_____Thinking of death is not fundamental to me.

223_____I find it difficult to think of death.
221_____I regret the thought of death.
219_____The thought of death is an awful thought.
217_____The thought of death is dreadful.
215_____The thought of death is traumatic.
213_____I hate the sound of the word death.
211_____The thought of death is outrageous.

The death attitude scale you have just taken in a pre-post fashion is a reliable and valid attitude scale. (For a detailed explanation of the validity and reliability of this scale, see Hardt, Dale V., "Development of an Investigating Instrument to Measure Attitudes Toward Death," *Journal of School Health*, 45, no. 2 [February, 1975], 96–99.)

To score, simply disregard the first number (2), place a decimal point between the two remaining numbers, and average the responses. The average will fall either on an attitude statement or between two attitude statements. Example: An individual checks items 237 (3.7), 235 (3.5), and 227 (2.7). By adding these together and dividing by the total number of items checked, an average of 3.3 is found. Hence, we can say that this person's attitude toward death at the time he or she took the test, is best described by statement 233, i.e., "I can accept the thought of death."

Score both the pretest and the post-test. If the pretest was favorable, i.e., 3.0 and up, there will probably be very little fluctuation in the post-test scale score. A fluctuation of .2 *either* up or down from your pretest to your post-test is not significant. We have found that people with favorable attitudes toward death do not tend to change their post attitude scale scores by very much.

If your pretest was lower than 3.0 we would expect to see a positive increase in death attitude scale score on your post-test. In fact, the lower your pretest, the more change we would expect to see. Hence, a 3.0 pretest might increase to a 3.2 or 3.4 while a 2.0 pretest would probably increase to a 2.8 or 3.0. This, of course, is dependent on your in-class experiences as well as on your involvement in this text. Furthermore, if the death of a loved one occurred after you took the pretest, we would expect the trauma of this experience to keep your post-test score low or bring it down from your pretest score if your pretest score was favorable to high (3.0 to 4.9).

In short, it has been demonstrated that one's attitude toward death can be improved, i.e., you can learn to accept death as a reality of living and be more comfortable with it. If you had a low to middle-of-the-road attitude toward death on the pretest, (1.1 to 3.0), hopefully your attitude has improved.

Index